Western Writing

Western Writing

Gerald W. Haslam, editor
California State College, Sonoma

UNIVERSITY OF NEW MEXICO PRESS

Albuquerque

Introduction copyright 1974 by the University of New Mexico Press.
All rights reserved. Manufactured in the United States of America.
Library of Congress Catalog Card Number 74-83389.
International Standard Book Number 0-8263-0353-6.
First edition.

Contents

1

Introduction:
Western Writers and the National Fantasy

GERALD W. HASLAM

Gerald W. Haslam is associate professor of English at California State College, Sonoma. He has published books and articles on a wide variety of American writers; his latest book is Afro-American Oral Literature, *and he is at work on a book about Jack Schaefer.*

Novelist Jack Schaefer, speaking of the historic West, noted that the effect of the frontier experience "was to unleash human energies, to throw into sharp focus human strengths and weaknesses, as rarely before in any period or place and never before on any comparable scale." Fortunately, there have been writers with both the sensitivity and the skill to capture the West. This book seeks to give readers some notion of what western writers have done, and why, offering clearer notions of what *West* really means.

During the nineteenth century, a time when the dangers of westering were compounded by a lurking fear of the unknown, the term *go west* became a synonym for *die*. Unfortunately for the many writers who have since sought to treat western experiences with seriousness and depth, going west in choice of material has been to "go west" in the eyes of critics. As late as 1955, Bernard DeVoto, himself a westerner, could lament not only that the West was "still looking for a serious novelist," but that it would "never find one."

With *The Ox-Bow Incident* (1940), of course, Walter Van Tilburg Clark had laid forever to rest serious doubts that great literature could come out of the West. This novel was so strong that many critics asserted that, although set in the West, it was not western literature. Such claims underline the role of national fantasy in the assessment of western writing, for common notions of the West have been more the products of fertile eastern imagina-

1

tions than of western experiences. If a story doesn't conform to the fantasy, it can't be western.

It was not the people of the frontier, for example, who read Calamity Jane and Buffalo Bill and Buck Taylor dime novels; rather those booklets entertained the masses in America's growing urban centers. The impact of dime novels published between 1860 and 1905 on the public consciousness is difficult to overestimate: they prepared people for the static popular westerns of this century. A relatively direct path may be traced from dime novels, through pulp magazines and western movies, to today's paperbacks and television oaters. Ned Buntline, Owen Wister, Clarence E. Mulford, Zane Grey, Max Brand, and Louis L'Amour created fantasies—sometimes brilliant fantasies—set in a mythical West, answering the needs of vast audiences. It is ironic that so many westerners have accepted popular stereotypes and sought to live up (or down) to them.

There is continuing debate over what the West and western experiences really are. Archibald MacLeish has called the West "a country in the mind," a compelling definition except that the West is also a real place or series of places, inhabited by real people. For a great many people the West is only a country in the mind, but for others it is, to paraphrase Tom Pilkington, their blood's country.

In this collection of essays, some of the finest western writers and scholars attempt to give some sense of how they have viewed their region, their history, and their craft. If they work at a depth and with a complexity of vision alien to popular notions fostered by formula westerns, the formula should be questioned.

The formula western, according to DeVoto, was clearly sketched by Owen Wister, an easterner whose experiences in the West were both brief and narrow. In *The Virginian* (1902), he lent greater credence to the fantasy prepared—or tapped—by dime novelists. He also missed completely the intense human and natural drama being played out all around him. While he detailed the adventures of a southern gentleman-turned-cowboy—"a slim young giant, more beautiful than pictures"—an epic was enacted, but Wister barely mentioned it: ". . . emigrants on their way from Black Hills to Oregon. A woman riding straddle, several other women, and any amount of children. Three slow crawling wagons ("prairie schooners") with their long teams. . . . A miserable population." In the opinion of many, Wister's work remains standard. DeVoto, in

"Birth of an Art," examines Wister's novel and its impact on both readers and writers. If DeVoto overestimates the importance of Wister's work, he does so reflecting its place in the national fantasy.

Perhaps the real West was too varied to be captured in a single formula. It moved and changed constantly throughout the nineteenth century, and literature has reflected such dynamism: James Fenimore Cooper described a hostile wilderness in the woodlands of the East, and Helen Hunt Jackson examined Mexican California; Ole Rölvaag's characters knew the vast loneliness of the Great Plains, while Jack Schaefer's most famous figure, Shane, symbolized the demise of the Palladin myth in the face of encroaching civilization; Andy Adams's cowpunchers worked hard at difficult, often dangerous chores, just as Frank Waters's individ-ualistic Indian worked to reintegrate himself with the dual truths of Tribe and Nature. Meanwhile, back at the ranch, Hopalong Cassidy and Hondo exterminated large numbers of human obstacles in melodramatic conflicts. It was immensely easier to project and accept a simple West that never was than to deal with the complex reality, especially when popular literature reinforced fantasy.

Moreover, during the very period when the West seemed most remote and unreal, American writing matured, allowing a huge literary gap between East and West to open. Transcendentalism gave way to naturalism as the harsh reality of urban life added a new dimension to our national literature. All the while, the West remained a distant reserve of static values and fantastic figures into which city dwellers could retreat. But other voices were rising, voices of those who had experienced the West, and who wanted something of its reality to be captured in literature.

In the work of writers such as Andy Adams and Eugene Manlove Rhodes, for example, the cattle kingdom escaped Wister's domina-tion. Their narratives demonstrated the truth of J. Frank Dobie's assertion: "Nothing is too trivial for art, but good art treats nothing in a trivial way." In *The Log of a Cowboy* (1903), Adams showed that trailing a herd of beeves, sans romance, was powerful literary stuff indeed; Rhodes, in *Pasó por Aquí* (1926), created a moving story around a less-than-heroic cowpoke. Adams and Rhodes were successful because they trusted their own experiences rather than the national cowboy fantasy. And, of course, so did Dobie, who could write movingly not only of the people of Texas but also of its coyotes, longhorns, and mustangs. Like Mary Austin, he came to

believe that a "sympathetic understanding based on both knowledge and feeling, of the land's features, both animate and
inanimate," was necessary in order truly to express the nature of a
place. In "The Writer and His Region," Dobie demonstrates his
own feel for his native Texas and suggests some general relationships between artists and their native soil. What makes a writer? It
is difficult to say completely, but Dobie certainly offers a leg up
when he suggests: "Writers will always be listening for the rhythms
of their living places."

Regionalism is nurtured by homogeneity as well as by an
identification with the nature of a region. Dobie had an advantage
not shared by most westerners: his native Texas, especially East
Texas, was relatively homogeneous, providing a great sense of
place. It was the western extension of the slave South, where mixed
European and African roots encountered Mexico; yet in spite of its
ethnic diversity, Texas harbored a strong sense of its own
uniqueness.

Most of the great West, however, was so varied that variety itself
seems to have been its major characteristic. We are faced with a
semantic dilemma: we say *West*, and consequently search for
common characteristics, when in fact we must deal with *Wests*.
We have assigned the West a permanent, ossified past without a
present. When western books are set in the present, critics seldom
call them western: the national myth allows the West only a past.
Indeed, critics have had problems dealing with western writing as
anything but myth. As Wallace Stegner observes, "Critics rarely
approach it from the near, or literary side. They mount it from the
right . . . and ride it hard as myth. . . ."

Because of the overwhelming power of the past, history and
historians loom large on the western landscape. Ultimately, all
historical writing is a form of literature—"a fable agreed on"—and
Stegner's close examination of narrative history, particularly that
written by Bernard DeVoto, offers insights into the process of
knowing and presenting a living past. Noting that DeVoto's novels
were unsuccessful, Stegner points out that the American West gave
him "a greater story and more colorful people than any he could
possibly have invented," noting further that "a historian cannot
invent drama but can only take advantage of it when he finds it."
The Stegner essay, "On the Writing of History," finally poses an
important question: When recreating a colorful, dramatic time, is

it possible to attain historical accuracy without somehow exploring the drama as well as the documents?

George Stewart tackles fundamental questions in his examination of regionalism in literature. His tighter definition demands that a work not only be "nominally located in the region, but also . . . derive actual substance from that location." Stewart points out the nature of regional writing and its pedagogical uses, summing matters up when he states:

> . . . all justification of the study of literature must rest upon a belief that it makes the individual a better citizen and a happier person. It seems to me that I have observed instances in which the study of regional literature has achieved this result, when perhaps the study of a more distant literature would not have done so.

A. B. Guthrie, Jr., explores the question of how and why western writers have used the past in his essay, "The Historical Novel," pointing out candidly that, as a novelist, he found the past "easier to deal with than the present." But he tempers his remarks by warning that what writers "need to remember, in the reconstruction of heroes, is just that no one ever was perfect." In recreating the time and place that were of special interest to him, the intermountain West of the nineteenth century, he sought "justice not in the sense of idolatry but of truth, of proportion." A quest for justice has motivated more than one serious western writer, for the very fantasy that has made much western art suspect has also obscured much of the region's varied history.

The western fantasy has prevailed to a large extent because it answers mythic human needs, needs transcending mere consciousness. Vardis Fisher, in "The Novelist and His Background," explores this deeper source of literary, and human, truth: "A novelist's background . . . is to be found less in the physical accidents of his life—in parents, neighbors, and geography—than in the past which produced the child." The past Fisher refers to is found "in all the centuries of our past history." A major part of a writer's background, then, "is the myths that have shaped him." Like Dobie, Fisher believes there is "intuitive wisdom" to be rediscovered, and much to be "unlearned," if we are again to see clearly. The great unsettled areas remaining in the West still offer some links to earth's wisdom.

Both John R. Milton ("The Novel in the American West") and J. Golden Taylor ("The Western Short Story") make specific judgments as they survey their subjects. Milton, in dealing with a vast panorama of western novels, confronts the omnipresent problem of myth versus reality, concluding that the "degree to which each Western novelist gives serious thought to this matter of myth determines in part his place in the hierarchy of the literary West." Though understandably dated—see especially Milton's placing of Stegner—the rating system suggested by Milton is thorough and thoughtful. Taylor ably demonstrates the heterogeneous nature of the West, the many Wests, making it especially clear that the cowboy is not the only notable figure available to Western writers. Like Milton's, Taylor's judgments are more than merely sound; they are the work of an expert. "My assumption all along," writes Taylor, "has been that one might reasonably expect that the literature of a region would have some resemblance to the lives of its people—that all life is the legitimate province of the literary artist." His selections and comments validate his assumption.

There have, of course, been westerners actively involved in evaluating western literature for a long time. Many have been historians interested in literature; the pervasiveness of the cowboy fantasy has led such critics to seek authenticity, among other qualities. In "The 'Western Story' as Literature," W. H. Hutchinson doesn't mince words in defining what he considers to be the West (". . . what you passed through to reach California or the Oregon Country"), in establishing the major divisions within western literature, and in choosing the best writers. After pointing out that many writers "knew the people who composed their market (audience) far better than they knew the people of whom they wrote . . . ," he prods his readers like range cattle toward a more critical view of what is authentic in western fiction.

Working on another level entirely, John Cawelti ("Prolegomena to the Western") defines and interprets "the Western formula."

David Lavender's "The Petrified West and the Writer" closes the circle, returning to the problems faced by serious western writers and stressing the problems inherent in the connotation of the word *western*. The major obstacle is, of course, the national fantasy: "The blockade, a familiar monolith vaster than Hoover Dam, is the stereotype now known as the horse opera." Lavender traces specific aspects of the blockade, offering suggestions and observations as to how the national fantasy will be transcended, suggesting finally that writers must look behind the West's compelling exterior, and dig "beneath the ash heaps of a century of foolish composition."

Western writers and scholars, like westerners generally, are a richly varied lot. They share a serious interest in the literature and history of their region, plus curiosity about the human condition, as the essays collected here (chosen by a panel of scholars) reveal. Written between the late 1940s and the early 1970s, these articles illustrate both the diversity of opinion and the rigor of thought that characterize the study of western American literature today. Western literary scholarship is a field as dynamic as its subject. Other essays might have been included, of course, but the necessity of narrowing this study to the general theme of western writing and regionalism, as well as the relative brevity of this volume, precluded more entries.

Western writers have struggled with the enormous power of fantasy—fantasy still widely held, indeed, widely sought—in their attempts to relate the awesome past to an elusive present. Many outstanding writers have dealt frontally with the Western present: Larry McMurtry, Amado Jesús Muro (Chester Seltzer), Leonard Gardner, William Stafford, John Steinbeck, Gary Snyder, Joan Didion, and Tomás Rivera, among others, have created a contemporary West relating to the past, but no writer has done more to create connections between the real *then* and the real *now* than Wallace Stegner.

The West has retained a national fascination throughout our history, so much so that many Americans remain unwilling to recognize its complexity, its continuing life along with its powerful past. Yet in the West there have been, and there are, writers and scholars who won't settle for mere fantasy. They have produced solid, imaginative, western literature based upon those powerful human experiences that transcend region without abandoning regional uniqueness. More importantly, readers all over the country are opening themselves to the real literature of the American West and, consequently, to the West itself.

"American history," historian Garrett Mattingly explained in a letter to his friend Bernard DeVoto, "is History in transition from an Atlantic to a Pacific phase." Perhaps the same might be said of American literature.

2

Birth of an Art

BERNARD DeVOTO

*Bernard DeVoto (1897–1955) was a distinguished American man of letters—
historian, critic, novelist, and editor.*

Some time ago I pointed out here that the obligatory scene of
horse opera, whether on the screen or the printed page, is what
Hollywood calls the walkdown. A sun god in leather pants, The
Hero, and his adversary, who represents Evil, approach each other
across an open space. The guns speak and The Hero, who has or has
not suffered a flesh wound, steps sideward into a girl's expectant
arms. This outcome solves all technical problems of the art form
and eliminates all problems of ethics, social sanction, and human
motivation. It is the climax of the fantasy that has kept the cowboy
story from becoming serious fiction. No doubt it is implicit in the
myth of the Old West and somebody else would have invented it if
Owen Wister hadn't. But he did invent it and the literary historian
can trace it to a simple caste snobbery.

The Cattle Kingdom, the era of large-scale cattle ranching on
the unfenced public range, ended in the late 1880s with the
collapse of inflationary financing, the increase of homesteading, the
ferocious winter called the Big Freeze, and the enforced adoption
of sensible ranch practices. Out in Wyoming a lot of wealthy
Eastern, English, and Scottish ranch owners who had been living on
capital without realizing it went broke and a lot more were going
broke. But an afterglow of the exuberant era lingered on so
pleasantly that the survivors could not understand that the world
had changed. A portion of Wyoming, Johnson County, had slipped
out of their personal control. It was filling up with small ranch
owners and even farmers, who were homesteading the public range

and sometimes stealing the Gentlemen's cows. Whereas the Gentlemen regarded the public range as theirs and had always had their foremen do the rustling. No convictions could be got in Johnson County, so it seemed a good idea to reverse a historical process with gunfire. A small army, composed of Gentlemen and hired Texas gunmen in about equal numbers, invaded Johnson County, to shoot it up. What got reversed was the army: Johnson County started shooting it up. It was saved in the last hundred feet of film by the U. S. Cavalry—just in time, the Gentlemen's Governor and their two Senators got the President of the United States and the Secretary of War out of bed to order the rescue. This small class conflict, whose surface is funnier than its roots and its sequel, is known in the texts as the Johnson County War. It occurred in 1892; almost every Hero of horse opera has had some connection with it.

Down to about 1880 the West in general and the cattle business in particular were realistically reported by the press. Fashions in journalism changed, however, and the roving correspondent began to find in cows and cowpokes a glamor which up to then had escaped his attention. He filled *Harper's, Scribner's,* and the *Century* with reports that gallantry was roaming the high plains and that the narrow code of the East would not hold in horizon land. There had arisen a person in a big hat whose grammar would seem deplorable in the drawing-room but who could see right through the drawing-room's shams. This type loved horses, respected good women, and when working at his trade performed heroisms that must evoke powerful admiration in the Eastern breast. He was muscular, he was brave, he told the truth, he stuck to his pardner, he scorned to shoot an unarmed enemy, and if Miss Mary Eleanor Wilkins' New England nun would consent to come West he would make her fruitful, lawfully.

Five years of ecstatic journalism prepared the soil for Owen Wister and he went West in 1885. He gratefully discovered that Wyoming had one's own kind in quantity, Philadelphians, Bostonians, New Yorkers of good clubs, younger sons, and titles. He visited their ranches—one of his earliest hosts was to be the Gentlemen's commanding general in 1892—and frequented their Cheyenne Club. He returned for other summers, shot big game, and got about widely. He met lots of the magazine correspondents' indigenous noblemen and watched them working at their glamorous trade. He met "desperadoes" too and other quaint, startling, and stock characters of the Cattle Kingdom. He listened to their talk. He also listened to the ideas of the Gentlemen.

Though he had a law degree Wister aspired to the arts and Wyoming crystallized his ambition. He wanted "to be the hand that once for all chronicled and laid bare the virtues and the vices of this extraordinary phase of American social progress." He was not to achieve this ambition—instead he invented horse opera—but it was an ambition of admirable artistic seriousness. We must attribute much significance to the episode that seems to have been decisive in making him a novelist.

He saw a Gentleman rancher, in a fit of insane rage, beat a horse with revolting cruelty and gouge out one of its eyes. An intolerable cruelty had been inflicted on Owen Wister too. This was Wyoming, that is to say Cibola; it was the abode of heroism and gallantry; yet this frightful, symbolic thing could happen. The country demanded interpretation in art. "No one has touched anywhere near it. . . . Its rise, its hysterical and unreal prosperity, and its disenchanting downfall, all this and its influence on the various sorts of human character that have been subjected to it—have not been touched on by a single writer that I, at least, have heard of. The fact is, it is quite worthy of Tolstoi or George Eliot or Dickens. Thackeray wouldn't do."

The last two sentences show that Wister understood what was required. The West was proper material for serious fiction, and he proposed to do what he could. But the preceding sentences reveal the inhibition: the West was what he had seen and heard of the afterglow of the Cattle Kingdom.

"I begin to conclude from five seasons of observation that life in this negligible, irresponsible wilderness tends to turn people shiftless, incompetent, and cruel. I noticed in 1885 and I notice today [1891] a sloth in doing anything and everything that is born of the deceitful ease with which makeshifts answer here." In this statement about the most difficult and laborious of our frontiers there is an exact equipoise between sight and blindness, perception and absurdity. Perhaps to a man of Wister's lineage and upbringing the eventual triumph of blindness was inevitable. Just before the flogging of the horse opened the heavens to him he had written, "On the way here [he was at the geographical center of Cibola, the Powder River] yesterday, passed emigrants on their way from

Black Hills to Oregon. A woman riding straddle, several other women, and any amount of children. Three slow crawling wagons ('prairie schooners') with their long teams. . . . A miserable population. These people, it seems, have been moving in this way pretty much all over the continent west of the Missouri, settling nowhere." And a sentence in a letter of 1894, after the war, "There's nothing makes this world seem so little evil as to meet good men in the humbler walks of life."

Well, he tried hard and he came nearer succeeding than, given the data, a critic could have predicted. And his good eye got no help from his own kind or from the arbiters of literature. *Harper's* for August 1892 carried the first of his stories about "the virtues and vices of this extraordinary land"; it was to publish everything else that came from his illumination. In January 1894 it ran "Balaam and Pedro," in which he described the blinding of the horse. *Harper's* was then edited by Henry Mills Alden, who thought of Wister's stories as mere vehicles for the art of Frederic Remington, and who had the most delicate sensibilities in American criticism. Alden did not permit Pedro's eye to be gouged out and he inflicted on the story such further softening that Wister was in despair. But a heavier blow called his whole intent into question, the disapproval of the friend whom he all but deified. Bowdlerized as the story was, it nevertheless shocked Theodore Roosevelt, who rebuked him for brutality and told him that the office of literature was to exalt and improve, not to disgust.

Wister did not restore the gouged eye, or apparently any other detail that Alden had excised, when he worked the story into *The Virginian*. But the book reveals that he could not use his good eye, either; its nature would not have been changed if he had embodied in it all the incidental brutalities he had heard about. He enclosed himself in the Old West; he was one of the artificers who made it up.

The Virginian is a novel published in 1902 but put together, with the joints left visible, from short stories he had published in *Harper's* during the 1890s. It was preceded in 1897 by a collection of short stories from the same period, but without the mythological Hero, called *Lin McLean*, which is important only as it shares the attributes of the later book. For in its earlier and its final form *The Virginian* created Western fiction—created the cowboy story, the horse-opera novel, the conventions, the clichés, the values, and the sun god. The cowboy story has seldom produced anything as good; apart from Gene Rhodes, it has not even tried to do anything different.

A fine comic sense informs much of the book. Also, I point out a surprising fact: the Virginian is permitted a casual and assured success in the seduction of women which the form has never since ventured to imitate. (The code holds that the cowboy reverences womanhood.) On the other hand, it is made clear that, though noble by virtue of his residence in Cibola, he has the humility to pattern his clothes, when not in costume, on the tailoring to be seen at the Cheyenne Club and to accept the literary taste of his schoolmarm, who is Miss Wilkins' New England nun. Finally, he has no name. Wister was unconsciously symbolizing the anonymity of the genre he was creating.

The fact which must be understood is that the themes of the book are from the Johnson County War. Wister scrambles his time sequences and in the last few pages says flatly that the events of that tragic farce are still to come. But they have already occurred—and to the Virginian. The novel is the Gentlemen's apologia. Its artistic problems originate in their purposes and ethics. It is an abiding literary irony: Wister fastened on horse opera and the myth of the Old West a dilemma whose only relevance, apart from the Cheyenne Club, is to the Main Line.

The Virginian is The Hero: a cowpoke righting wrongs, doing justice, avenging injury, triumphing over perils, eradicating evil, and shooting people. Shooting bad people. Shooting Johnson County "rustlers"; that is, quite uncultivated persons who have small land-holdings and small herds. He is one of those "good men in the humbler walks of life" who "make this world seem so little evil." But the Old West is fervently democratic and he can rise to equal status with the Gentlemen. As an employee of one of them, he adopts the values of the well-born and cultivates their manners. Miss Mary Stark Wood, of one of those gracious houses on Monument Avenue in Bennington, encourages him to read elevating books and he improves his spelling by himself. It is to be said further that the Episcopal Bishop of Wyoming admires him—I believe that the see was then a mission and so the Bishop's acceptance of murder as a folkway may be regarded as a compromise necessary to the conversion of the heathen. Having patterned himself on the Gentlemen and executed their justice, the

Virginian marries Miss Wood, becomes a ranch owner, acquires coal lands, makes a fortune, and so moves naturally among the Frewens, Gardiners, Careys, Teschemachers, and Warrens.

Till he went to work for Judge Henry the Virginian was a ramblin' cowboy and so, necessarily in the Old West, had shot an unspecified number of men. But he is able to tell Miss Wood's mother that he has "never killed for pleasure or profit" and is not "one of that kind, always preferring peace." Here is the bedrock reason why *The Virginian* and the genre it created were prohibited from being serious fiction. The declaration was true as Wister understood it. Before and during the Johnson County War, and after it too, the Gentlemen both killed and hired killing for profit, but murder in the interest of a master class is not unethical. The declaration sets forth another necessity: The Hero must be a goodie, he must conquer Evil. He acquires his Adversary, and the genre acquires its type villain, in Trampas, to whom in the second chapter he speaks the line that has become immortal, "When you call me that, smile." (Spatial limitations make the stage unfit for horse opera or it might have had stern competition from a line in "The Great Divide," by William Vaughn Moody, which was being taught as the best American play when I was an undergraduate. Just before the final curtain the Eastern heroine compresses the Old West into a single sentence, spoken to The Hero, "Teach me to live as you do.")

Trampas is a rustler, so eventually The Hero must kill him; another necessity has been established. And the form acquires another device that is little less than universal when Miss Wood saves The Hero's life—after he has been shot by Indians, which is first-rate shooting for Wyoming in the 1890s.

Rustlers are preying on the Gentlemen's herds and must be killed. One of them is, or rather once was, The Hero's best friend, his partner. But The Hero has to help lynch him in protection of the Gentlemen's commercial hegemony. The failure of horse opera to become serious fiction pivots on this necessity and on Judge Henry's explanation of it to Miss Wood. I repeat that Wister tried hard, and he tried hardest here, confronting what is in artistic terms the problem of his novel. He tried honestly and conscientiously to solve it as an artist, but he could not make the grade.

It turns out that in one part of the Old West, or Cibola, small property owners have taken the mechanisms of government away from the Gentlemen. The Gentlemen have no choice but to replace them with murder. Judge Henry tells Miss Wood that murder is all right, it is in accordance with the strictest principles of our republican forms and with the evolution of law in society, when it is done—or in this instance hired—by Gentlemen of a certain economic station. Miss Wood has little difficulty believing him, for she might have been the heroine of "The Great Divide," but The Hero must grapple with an inner conflict. For obeying a major provision of the code requires him to violate a provision that had not previously been understood to be a lesser one. There was no getting away from the fact that Steve, the hanged baddie, had been his partner; it is a bitter thing that property must transcend not only law but friendship too. Still there is an alleviation: Steve dies game.

The basic dilemma of horse opera would not have existed if Wister had examined what had been happening when the courts of Laramie County, as distinguished from Johnson County, tried a sheepman or a small cattle rancher, that is a baddie, who was accused of committing a tort against a Gentleman. He discussed this commonplace every time he visited a friend or spent an hour at the Cheyenne Club. But these were persons of substance and breeding and it was inevitable for Wister, as it has remained necessary for his genre, to romanticize the use of murder as a business method.

It was the Old West that supplied the Virginian as Hero with his past, stage properties, mannerisms, and code. It was the art of fiction that set up as the central action of the book the pursuit and lynching of Steve. But it was the vanishing hegemony of the Gentlemen that provided the evasion and capitulation, Judge Henry's lecture on the place of law in society. That did it. Wister would not be the West's Tolstoi nor even its unsuitable Thackeray, and the literary form called horse opera had been invented. He went on to give the form its supreme effect.

Having saved The Hero's life and accepted his employer's position on murder as an economic instrument, Miss Mary Stark Wood of the patrician East plights him her troth. (The Old West will supply ennobling landscapes for the honeymoon; besides tailoring, the Harvard Club of New York will supply an approved kind of ring.) The two set off for town, where the Bishop of Wyoming will marry them, but on the way they see Trampas. The

Hero must kill the baddie or the baddie will kill him. (The code will not permit him to have the baddie jailed.) A problem remains: what explanation shall he give his bride? As these contrivances are worked out, somewhere along the way motive as a component of human behavior, occasionally present up to now, makes its final exit from horse opera. It has never yet returned.

Meeting the Bishop of Wyoming, The Hero listens to the Christian's advice to run away for at least his wedding night, rejects it, and says good-by, the Bishop murmuring as he leaves, "God bless him! God bless him!" Though Miss Wood has divined what is to come, he tells her and will not yield when she falls on her knees and begs him "For my sake. For my sake." So, " 'I have no right to kiss you any more,' he said. And then before his desire could break him down from this he was gone and she was alone."

The Hero's friends make sure that no minor baddie will do the job for Trampas. "Then he walked out into the open, watching." His friends follow at a proper distance, "because it was known that Shorty [an earlier victim of Trampas'] had been shot from behind." Presently, "A wind seemed to blow his sleeve off his arm and he replied to it, and saw Trampas pitch forward. He saw Trampas raise his arm from the ground and fall again and lie there, this time still. A little smoke was rising from the pistol on the ground, and he looked at his own and saw the smoke flowing upward out of it. 'I expect that's all,' he said aloud."

That is the first walkdown. In a moment The Hero steps into Miss Wood's arms. She thanks God that he has killed Trampas. And what you see disappearing over the horizon into the mirage of the Old West is an art form that might possibly have given us some true reports on and understanding of one segment of American experience but that is still looking for a serious novelist. And will never find one.

3

The Writer and His Region

J. FRANK DOBIE

*J. Frank Dobie (1888–1964) taught for many years at the University of Texas.
The author of numerous books and articles, he was considered a dean of
southwestern writers.*

Good writing about any region is good only to the extent that it
has universal appeal. Texans are the only "race of people" known
to anthropologists who do not depend upon breeding for propaga-
tion. Like princes and lords, they can be made by "breath," plus a
big white hat—which comparatively few Texans wear. A beef stew
by a cook in San Antonio, Texas, may have a different flavor from
that of a beef stew cooked in Pittsburgh, Pennsylvania, but the
essential substances of potatoes and onions, with some suggestion of
beef, are about the same, and geography has no effect on their
digestibility.

A writer—a regional writer, if that term means anything—will
whenever he matures exercise the critical faculty. I mean in the
Matthew Arnold sense of appraisal rather than of praise, or, for that
matter, of absolute condemnation. Understanding and sympathy
are not eulogy. Mere glorification is on the same intellectual level
as silver tongues and juke box music.

In using that word *intellectual,* one lays himself liable to the
accusation of having forsaken democracy. For all that, "fundamental brainwork" is behind every respect-worthy piece of writing,
whether it be a lightsome lyric that seems as careless as a redbird's
flit or a formal epic, an impressionistic essay or a great novel that
measures the depth of human destiny. Nonintellectual literature is
as nonexistent as education without mental discipline. Billboards

First published in the *Southwest Review,* Spring 1950, this article was based on an address
delivered by the author to the Texas Institute of Letters in 1949. Reprinted by permission of
Mrs. Bertha Dobie and the *Southwest Review.*

along the highways of Texas advertise certain towns and cities as "cultural centers." No chamber of commerce, of course, would consider advertising an intellectual center—not because it does not exist. The culture of a nineteenth-century finishing school for young ladies was divorced from intellect, but a true culture, beyond the sociological use of the word, is always informed by intellect. The American populace has been taught to believe that the more intellectual a professor is, the less common sense he has; nevertheless, if American democracy is preserved it will be preserved by thought and not by physics.

Editors of all but a few magazines of the country and publishers of most of the daily newspapers cry out for brightness and vitality and at the same time shut out critical ideas. They want intellect, but want it petrified. Happily, the publishers of books have not yet reached that form of delusion. In an article entitled "What Ideas Are Safe?" in the *Saturday Review of Literature* for November 5, 1949, Henry Steele Commager says:

> If we establish a standard of safe thinking, we will end up with no thinking at all. . . . We cannot . . . have thought half slave and half free. . . . A nation which, in the name of loyalty or of patriotism or of any sincere and high-sounding ideal, discourages criticism and dissent, and puts a premium on acquiescence and conformity, is headed for disaster.

Unless a writer feels free, things will not come to him, he cannot burgeon on any subject whatsoever.

One hundred and fifteen years ago Davy Crockett's Autobiography was published. It is one of the primary social documents of America. It is as much Davy Crockett, whether going ahead after bears in a Tennessee canebrake or going ahead after General Andrew Jackson in Congress, as the equally plain but also urbane Autobiography of Franklin is Benjamin Franklin. It is undiluted regionalism. It is provincial not only in subject but in point of view.

No provincial mind of this day could possibly write an autobiography or any other kind of book co-ordinate in value with Crockett's "classic in homespun." In his time, Crockett could exercise intelligence and still retain his provincial point of view. Provincialism was in the air over his land. In these changed times, something in the ambient air prevents any active intelligence from being unconscious of lands, peoples, struggles far beyond any province.

Not long after the Civil War, in Harris County, Texas, my father heard a bayou-billy yell out:

Whoopee! Raised in a canebrake and suckled by a she-bear!
The click of a sixshooter is music to my ear!
The further up the creek you go, the worse they git,
And I come from the head of it! Whoopee!

If it were now possible to find some section of country so far up above the forks of the creek that the owls mate there with the chickens, and if this section could send to Congress one of its provincials untainted by the outside world, he would, if at all intelligent, soon after arriving on Capitol Hill become aware of interdependencies between his remote province and the rest of the world.

Biographies of regional characters, stories turning on local customs, novels based on an isolated society, books of history and fiction going back to provincial simplicity will go on being written and published. But I do not believe it possible that a good one will henceforth come from a mind that is regional in outlook, a mind that does not in outlook transcend the region on which it is focused. This is not to imply that the processes of evolution have brought all parts of the world into such interrelationships that a writer cannot depict the manners and morals of a community up Owl Hoot Creek without enmeshing it with the complexities of Lake Success. Awareness of other times and other wheres, not insistence on that awareness, is the requisite. James M. Barrie said that he could not write a play until he got his people off on a kind of island, but had he not known about the mainland he could never have delighted us with the islanders—islanders, after all, for the night only. Patriotism of the right kind is still a fine thing; but, despite all gulfs, canyons, and curtains that separate nations, those nations and their provinces are all increasingly interrelated.

No sharp line of time or space, like that separating one century from another or the territory of one nation from that of another, can delimit the boundaries of any region to which any regionalist lays claim. Mastership, for instance, of certain locutions peculiar to the Southwest will take their user to the Aztecs, to Spain, and to the border of ballads and Sir Walter Scott's romances. I found that I could not comprehend the coyote as animal hero of Pueblo and Plains Indians apart from the Reynard of Aesop and Chaucer.

In a noble opinion respecting censorship and freedom of the press, handed down on March 18, 1949, Judge Curtis Bok of Pennsylvania said:

> It is no longer possible that free speech be guaranteed Federally and denied locally; under modern methods of instantaneous communication such a discrepancy makes no sense. . . . What is said in Pennsylvania may clarify an issue in California, and what is suppressed in California may leave us the worse in Pennsylvania. Unless a restriction on free speech be of national validity, it can no longer have any local validity whatever.

Among the qualities that any good regional writer has in common with other good writers of all places and times is intellectual integrity. Having it does not obligate him to speak out on all issues or, indeed, on any issue. He alone is to judge whether he will continue to sport with Amaryllis in the shade or forsake her to write his own Areopagitica. Intellectual integrity expresses itself in the tune as well as in argument, in choice of words—words honest and precise—as well as in ideas, in fidelity to human nature and the flowers of the fields as well as to principles, in facts reported more than in deductions proposed. Though a writer write on something as innocuous as the white snails that crawl up broomweed stalks and that roadrunners carry to certain rocks to crack and eat, his intellectual integrity, if he has it, will infuse the subject.

Nothing is too trivial for art, but good art treats nothing in a trivial way. Nothing is too provincial for the regional writer, but he cannot be provincial-minded toward it. Being provincial-minded may make him a typical provincial; it will prevent him from being a representative or skilful interpreter. Horace Greeley said that when the rules of the English language got in his way, they did not stand a chance. We may be sure that if by violating the rules of syntax Horace Greeley sometimes added forcefulness to his editorials, he violated them deliberately and not in ignorance. Luminosity is not stumbled into. The richly savored and deliciously unlettered speech of Thomas Hardy's rustics—the very cream of rusticity—was the creation of a master architect who had looked out over the ranges of fated mankind and looked also into hell. Thomas Hardy's ashes were placed in Westminster Abbey, but his heart, in accordance with a provision of his will, was buried in the churchyard of his own village.

I have never tried to define regionalism. Its blanket has been put over a great deal of worthless writing. Robert Frost has approached a satisfying conception. "The land is always in my bones," he said—the land of rock fences. But, "I am not a regionalist. I am a realmist. I write about realms of democracy and realms of the spirit." Those realms include The Woodpile, The Grindstone, Blueberries, Birches, and many other features of the land North of Boston.

To an extent, any writer anywhere must make his own world, no matter whether in fiction or nonfiction, prose or poetry. He must make something out of his subject. What he makes depends upon his creative power, integrated with a sense of form. The popular restriction of creative writing to fiction and verse is illogical. Carl Sandburg's life of Lincoln is immeasurably more creative in form and substance than his fanciful *Potato Face*. Intense exercise of this creative power sets, in a way, the writer apart from the life he is trying to sublimate. Becoming a Philistine will not enable a man to interpret Philistinism, though Philistines who own big presses think so. Sinclair Lewis knew Babbitt as Babbitt could never know either himself or Sinclair Lewis.

There is no higher form of art and, therefore, no higher form of patriotism than translating the features of the patria into forms of dignity, beauty, and nobility. I would not trade Roy Bedichek's chapters on the mockingbird for all the essays and orations that the Fourth of July has occasioned during the past one hundred and seventy-five years.

In an essay on "The Spirit of the Place," D. H. Lawrence—whom I do not consider a very wise soul but who sometimes penetrated truth—said: "Men are free when they are in a living homeland, not when they are straying and breaking away." What is the spirit, the tempo, the rhythm of this plot of earth to which we belong and as writers endeavor to express? Often it seems that the essential spirit has been run over and killed. But nature is as inexorable, as passionless, and as patient in revenge as she is in fidelity to "the heart that loves her." In the long run, she cannot be betrayed by man; in the long run, man can betray only himself by not harmonizing with her.

Wise Mary Austin, who was a true prophet of the Land of Little Rain, held that "no man has ever really entered into the heart of any country until he has adopted or made up myths about its familiar objects"; until, that is, he has achieved a sympathetic understanding, based on both knowledge and feeling, of the land's features, animate as well as inanimate. As an interpreter of the spirit of the Southwest, John Joseph Mathews of the Osages and the blackjacks belongs in the small company that Mary Austin heads. The sage of his *Sundown* says, talking to his own people:

> You are Indian. You are part of this earth here like trees, like rabbit, like birds. Our people built their lodges here. That which came out of ground into their feet and over their bodies into their hands, they put into making of their lodges. They made songs out of that which came out of ground into their bodies. Those lodges were good and beautiful. Those songs were good and beautiful. . . . White man came out of ground across the sea. His thoughts are good across the sea. His houses are beautiful across the sea, I believe. His houses are ugly here because they did not come out of this earth.

Probably few Americans, as we call ourselves, will ever belong to the land as intimately as some of the American Indians belonged, will ever let the rhythms of the earth—Mary Austin's phrase—so seep into their natures. Yet not all the houses are as ugly as they were. The more modern architecture becomes, the more do dwellings seem to "come out of this earth." The other kind of architecture and the way of life represented by that other kind of architecture put population into fast-running cars and faster-flying airplanes. Man, however, has no prospect of a machine that will fly him away from himself. Though he were to become so entirely a product of machinery that he could subsist on Coca-Cola and protein tablets, they still come from the earth that he came from and is bound to. Actually, hardly an individual wants to escape the earth, but regard the mass of us: We spend our prime energies building cities and then spend what's left trying to escape the progress we have made. Many a time while paying four or five dollars for a two-dollar noisy hotel room I have wished that by doubling the price I could be transported to a blanket on mesquite grass somewhere where the crickets chirp. Happiness is a state of being in harmony with one's environment.

During World War I Frederick Russell Burnham, as he tells in *Scouting on Two Continents,* was searching for manganese in the mountains of California. He grubstaked various old prospectors to search. One day one of them on a high mountain amid desert desolation, after sitting a long while in silence as he was wont to sit, leaned toward Burnham and said: "The mountains are all whispering to me. If I could only understand."

Writers will always be listening for the rhythms of their living places. Whatever the rhythm of our part of the earth is, not one of us will catch it unless we can sometimes sit in "wise passiveness" and hear "tidings of invisible things."

The tidings we are after are both visible and invisible, both audible and inaudible. It is not easy to get the right words, but getting them calls for less acuteness than getting the essential rhythm. One may read *Deserts on the March* and study mountains of documents on erosion, restoration of grasses, and plant ecology and thereby become a useful technician, but the rhythm of the grasses and of the soil that grows them cannot be documented.

Much noise has made it retreat. The mass productions of press, radio, and film have made the West a place of roaring guns, men with tense grim tones, and action—action always. You have to go out into remoteness to find the rhythms that belong.

Sam Galloway, O. Henry's "Last of the Troubadours," never "sat up when he could lie down and never stood when he could sit." He was a great hand to linger. For the cowman in Andy Adams' novel there was always "ample time." Frederic Remington painted many pictures of Western action, but he never painted an action picture that catches the Spirit of the Place as does a little-known one of his called "The Blue Bird." It shows an Indian who has been walking in the forest standing with hands raised in a kind of prayer of thankfulness at sight of the first bluebird of spring.

For me at least, the buzzard expresses better the tempo of the land than any airplane trying to run him down. One time, as an old Negro tale tells, a buzzard was sailing slow, around and around, in great circles high up in the air.

A hawk arrowing by him paused to say, "What you waiting round for, Brother Buzzard?"

"I'm awaiting the will of God," the buzzard replied, and he sailed on slow and majestical.

After a while the hawk shot by again. "Come with me," he said. "Let's get going and catch some meat."

"No, I thank you," the buzzard said. "I await the will of God." He sailed on as easy as a cottonwood leaf floating on glass-smooth water.

A third time the hawk shot into the buzzard's circle. "Old Slow Thing," he said, "I'm going to show you how to get meat. See that mockingbird perched way down yonder on that sharp stob of the dead tree?"

"I see," said the buzzard. "In the sand right under the mockingbird a thousand-legs is curled up."

"Now, Brother Buzzard, watch me." And the hawk bulleted straight for the mockingbird.

But somehow he missed his aim. Just as he was at the target, the mockingbird flew and the hawk rammed his breast against the stob of the dead tree. He fell to the ground dead. The buzzard, still unhurried, began to shorten the circle of his flight. Slowly, slowly, he spiraled groundward. He had awaited the will of God.

Two kinds of people of this world have each with their kind deep kinships, no matter what language they speak or in what latitude they live: people with cultivated minds and people of the soil. An old Indian of Tutepec in Oaxaca had the rhythm that belongs to all places where shade is gracious. Down there in Oaxaca every man's house has a *ramada* (a shed), and every *ramada* is hung with hammocks. I had come to know this old Indian and one afternoon as I approached his house he arose from his hammock to welcome me. He motioned me to the hammock beside his, and as we reclined in harmony, he said, "Señor, isn't God good! He gives us the nights to sleep in and the days to rest in."

Tempo, like anything else, can be overstressed. The writer of a region can never know enough about it. He has to know how far "a fur piece" is and how long "after a while" may be. He has to know how deep the shadow on the rock lies and sometimes what "maybe so" denies. He has to know so much that as he writes he will be constantly obliged to exercise that most difficult of arts—the "art of omission."

Only sympathy, acting through knowledge, can unlock for him some of the knowable, though invisible, realities. Two skilful writers are now writing the history of a certain oil company. This company has taken a great deal of oil from the old Tom O'Connor ranch on the Texas coast. Oil is a tremendous fact in the economy of the world. A kind of oil culture dominates Texas with more force than cattle ever dominated it. It is mighty. It is a mighty subject for writing, but only the devil would want to pipe it into the green pastures of heaven. After all the oil has been pumped from beneath the surface of O'Connor land, the grasses will still be green there and wave in the Gulf breeze as they waved thousands of years before Cabeza de Vaca walked across them. The history of the oil company will contain many facts. It can hardly be expected to suggest the sympathy for the land that Tom O'Connor had.

He had deeds to scores of sections of lands and he owned ten thousand cattle on the prairies and in the brush, and now Old Tom O'Connor could no longer ride across the seas of grass and watch his cattle thrive. One day he told his boss, Pat Lambert, to take all hands out early next morning and bring in the biggest herd they could gather. To Pat Lambert, early morning always meant by four o'clock. After he and his hands had ridden out a ways, they stopped to wait for daylight. They rode hard and they rode far, and about an hour before sundown they drove a vast herd of mixed cattle to the holding and cutting grounds not far from the O'Connor ranch house. Bulls were challenging, cows were bawling, steers and stags were bellowing, calves were bleating. Heifers, yearlings, old moss-horned steers, all ages of cattle of both sexes, were milling about, their blended voices rising above the dust from their hoofs.

While some of the hands held the herd and others changed horses, Pat Lambert went into the room where Tom O'Connor lay on his bed.

"We made a big drag, Mr. Tom," he said.

"I hear them," Tom O'Connor replied. His voice was thin.

"What do you want me to do with them, Mr. Tom?"

"Nothing. Just hold them there. I'm dying, Pat, and I want to go out with natural music in my ears."

4

On the Writing of History

WALLACE STEGNER

Wallace Stegner was director of the creative writing program at Stanford until his retirement in 1971. He is a distinguished novelist and essayist.

Recently I asked a doctoral candidate who was embarking on a history of Berlin since World War II if he intended to dramatize the personalities and events of those twenty years. Was he going to write an analysis or a story? How would his book be affected if, as he uncovered his material, he came upon people who played protagonist and antagonist, embodying in themselves significant forces of the cold war? How would he handle the challenges and confrontations, the suspense, the climactic scenes? Clearly he would encounter such things, for how could he overlook Adenauer, Willi Brandt, Walter Ulbricht, the jockeyings for political advantage, the tie-ups on the Autobahn, the airlift, the mass flight, the Wall? But when I asked my question he looked at me, and so did some of the eminent historians on his committee, with a slight quizzical smile. I was thinking like a journalist or a novelist, not like a historian. He had not studied, and they had not trained him, to approach his dissertation in any such mood as that. They had trained him to probe for cause and consequence, to exhaust sources, to analyze, to generalize from tested facts. Pretty obviously they considered the analytical approach the only intellectually respectable one. Obviously they thought that treating those explosive two decades as drama would endanger the dependability of the result. They did not want him producing something like Leon Uris' *Armageddon.*

In holding him to an intellectually rigorous method they were, beyond all question, sound. But I think they dismissed too lightly an approach that would have been, for that particular segment of

From *The American West* Magazine, Fall 1965, © copyright 1965 by the American West Publishing Company, Palo Alto, California. Reprinted by permission of the publisher.

25

history, the most proper one. The postwar history of Berlin will not
be properly written until it is narrated. A *good* book on Berlin may
be a pastiche of communiques, conferences, policies, ultimatums,
and abstract forces. The *great* book on Berlin is going to be a sort of
Iliad, a story that dramatizes a power struggle in terms of the men
who waged it. Which does not mean at all that it will be
intellectually deficient.

History's truth is truth to fact, to what happened. "If you take
truth from History," says Polybius, "what is left but an improfitable
tale?" And what is an improfitable tale but fiction, whose truth is
not truth to fact but truth to plausibility? Yet it is not the presence
of dramatic narrative that makes false history false. Falseness
derives from inadequate or inaccurate information, faulty research,
neglected resources, bias, bad judgment, misleading implication,
and these afflict the expository among us about as often as they
afflict the narrative. It is true that the excitement of story-telling,
like the excitement of phrase-making, often tempts a writer into
misrepresentation. But the excitement of analysis, the excitement
of generalization, can do the same; and the laudable lust for
absolute accuracy can lead to dullness, can cause a man to proffer a
set of notes instead of a finished book, as if one did not write
history, but collected it.

Any method has its dangers. The solution is not to repudiate both
generalization and dramatization, both the accurate and the vivid,
and sit inert in the middle of one's virtue. Neither is anything
gained by pretending that all narrative historians write better than
expository historians, for clearly some narrative historians write
badly and many expository historians write extremely well. Speaking as an amateur, I should guess that the trick is to make the twin
cutting tools of sound research and a sense of the dramatic work
together like scissor blades.

I have heard of a university history department which was
offered a visiting historian noted for his grace of style. The idea of
the donor was to let him have a salutary effect on the quality of the
local historical prose. The department refused him, saying in effect,
Thank you, no, we'll haggle along with our own dull saw. If they
had taken him, he might have taught them that well-written
history does not have to be inaccurate, and he might have learned
from them that not all dull history is dependable. Maybe both
would have learned that the dramatizing of legitimately dramatic

true events does not necessarily falsify them, nor need it leave their meaning ambiguous.

Dramatic narrative is simply one means by which a historian can make a point vividly. To imagine historiography without this possibility is like imagining Christ without His parables, or Abraham Lincoln without his anecdotes.

o   o   o

Calliope and Clio are not identical twins, but they *are* sisters. History, a fable agreed on, is not a science but a branch of literature, an artifact made by artificers and sometimes by artists. Like fiction, it has only persons, places, and events to work with, and like fiction it may present them either in summary or in dramatic scene. Conversely, fiction, even fantastic fiction, reflects so much of the society that produces it that it may have an almost-historical value as record. Objective and sociological novels come very close to history, the difference being principally that history reports the actual, fiction the typical. Thus *An American Tragedy*, working out what Dreiser felt to be a characteristic American fate, was built on the extensive study of real murder trials, and in its text—transporting them bodily from real to make-believe—it incorporates many details and several documents from the case of Chester Gillette, who was convicted and executed for the murder of his girl in upstate New York in 1906.

That transposition of the actual into the fictional is only one instance of a common process. There is a whole middle ground between fiction and history. So-called historical fiction, which transposes the fictional into the actual, may have every degree of historical authenticity up to the highest, while things called history and biography may be treated with so little of the historian's responsibility to fact that they amount to frauds. There are respectable books all across the spectrum, but it is important that they be called what they are, and do not pretend to be what they are not.

I defend the middle ground as one who has strayed there several times—in *The Preacher and the Slave, Beyond the Hundredth Meridian, The Gathering of Zion*, and *Wolf Willow*. I doubt that any of those books fuses fiction and history with total success, but each has shown me a different possibility. Any librarian would catalogue the first as a novel, the second as a biography, the third as history. The fourth might give her classificatory heartburn. But at least in the matter of method and approach I am prepared to defend them all.

The Preacher and the Slave, an account of the life and death of the IWW martyr Joe Hill, is a novel: it has a novel's intentions and takes a novel's liberties. As necessary, I invented characters, scenes, motivations, dialogue, and though Hill's execution gave me an inescapable ending, I bent the approach to that conclusion as seemed to me needful. But the bending that seemed needful was also imposed on me, in a way, for I had spent four or five years collecting documentary and other evidence on both Joe Hill and the IWW, had hunted down seven or eight people who had known the elusive Joe Hill in life, had studied the trial transcript and many newspaper files, had talked with the family of the two men Hill was accused of murdering, and with the sheriff who conducted the execution by firing squad, with the Wobbly editor who arranged Hill's public funeral in Chicago, and with balladeers who had written Joe Hill songs. I had attended IWW martyr meetings. I had gotten the warden of the Utah State Penitentiary to walk me through a mock execution so that I would know imaginatively how a condemned and blindfolded man might feel in the very soles of his feet his progress toward death down iron stairs, across paved courtyard, into cindered alley to the chair with the bullet-battered backstop.

That is, I took every bit as much pains as I would have taken if I had intended to write a history, and I think that when I started to write I knew as much IWW history as anybody in the world and could judge its passions and its ambiguities almost as impartially. Also, I blended the fictional and the documentary as Dreiser had done. The last section utilizes actual letters to and from Joe Hill, some of the trial records, some of the record of a hearing before the pardon board, some of Joe Hill's songs written in prison. A pretty historical book, in its way. Nevertheless, I took pains in a foreword to label it "an act of the imagination," which is what I wanted it to be.

In *Beyond the Hundredth Meridian* I had no such fictional aim. The book is a biography of Major John Wesley Powell, which incorporates much of the history of the western surveys and of the formation of several Washington bureaus. Much of it is as expository as it could well be. But all the expository history rests upon an opening section that is nearly pure narrative, pure adventure story: the account of Powell's first expedition down the Green and Colorado rivers in 1869. In giving that narrative nearly a third of the book, I may have been warping some abstract and ideal proportion, but I invented nothing, not even the feelings of the men I was following. I only exploited what their journals and letters offered me, and tried to imagine my way into their situation through my own knowledge of the canyons. Unlike the novelist, a historian cannot invent drama but can only take advantage of it when he finds it. In this book I wanted to be a historian.

Invention was not a possibility in *The Gathering of Zion*, either, since my intention was to write the history of the Mormon migration in the terms of the people who made it. Admittedly the aim was selective, since it left out much doctrinal, hierarchic, and political material, but within its limitations I wanted it to be as accurate as I could make it. I was much less interested in the doctrinal and political causes of this march than in the march itself, and in what faith did to the people who held it. In *The Preacher and the Slave* I had been after the personality of a rebel. I had started out by getting interested in *songs* that men had died to. Here on the Mormon Trail was a *faith* that people had died for.

My intention in *The Gathering of Zion* was clearly novelistic in its emphasis on human interest, but historical in that I wanted to be faithful to fact and record. Because I was after visceral history, I gave myself an extensive Parkman-esque exposure to the geography and weather of the trail; and I stuck close to the dust and storms and exhaustion and trials of faith reflected in the letters and journals of a wide range of people. Because this subject had been treated too often by partisans full of the zeal of attack or defense, I tried to exhaust these journal sources and not to stray from them. It is obvious from the amount of space I gave to the hegira from Nauvoo, the pioneer trip to Salt Lake Valley, and the tragic handcart episode that I was seizing every chance to dramatize—seizing, in fact, the same events that the Mormon imagination had already built into myths. Where the events of the migration were not especially dramatic, I told them in summary. So except for a few chapters, this is essentially narrative history. But it *is* history, if I understand the term.

My own opinion is that *Wolf Willow* ought to be called history too, though it is nearly a third reminiscence and more than a third fiction. The publishers solved the problem by subtitling it, "A History, a Story, and a Memory." But I hope that it is one thing, not three, and its dominant impulse was historical. Having grown up literally without history, in a place where human actions had not been formally remembered and recorded, I developed long after I left there the ambition to write at least the beginning of the history of those hills in southern Saskatchewan where the buffalo and the Plains Indians came to their end as a culture and a force. I wanted to be the Herodotus of the Cypress Hills. Like that other father of history, I found the documentation thin—a scrap or two in the *Jesuit Relations*, a bit in *Le Métis Canadien*, a few Hudson's Bay records and reminiscences, some newspaper accounts of the Cypress Hills Massacre and its aftermath, something about Sitting Bull, something about the Mounted Police, some recollections of old-timers, one continuous local newspaper file beginning in 1914. But I had lived in the hills myself, and my memories were sharp. It seemed legitimate, as a means of realizing the country for readers, to put my remembering senses into the book, and my own family's experiences. And when I came to write about the open-range cattle industry, I was irresistibly driven to write it as fiction, as a typical story rather than as an expository summary. I thought I could get more truth into a slightly fictionalized story of the winter that killed the cattle industry on the northern plains than I could into any summary. So I wrote that section as three connected stories, a sort of broken novel. Later I took out the middle one, a yarn called "The Wolfer," for entirely literary reasons: it was told in the first person by a Mounted Policeman, and it intruded a disturbingly subjective "voice" into a book that was already discontinuous enough. Unlike fiction, history can have only one voice, the historian's.

                              o   o   o

Those are only four of many possible combinations that lie between the poles of history and fiction. Whatever the combination, I am positive that the novelist's skill with scene, character, and symbol may be used, not to cheapen history but to enhance it. One way of understanding something is to see it recreated—a playback. The great romantic historians, Bancroft, Motley, Prescott, and Parkman, freely used such skills, and they gravitated naturally toward the heroic subjects that permitted heroic treatment. Their histories are not to be understood out of the context that includes Sir Walter Scott. As Davis Levin has pointed out, their histories are not so much record as romantic art. Obviously there is every justification for the kind of history that preserves and records, but history as romantic art—or realistic art, for that matter—is not entirely the province of lesser lady novelists and popularizers. As a modern instance of the meeting of a great subject and a great talent I cite you Bernard DeVoto.

It would have frustrated DeVoto, who tried long and hard to be a novelist, to know that his essays and especially his histories would outlast his novels. But it is true that the talents which labor and overheat in the novels run smooth and cool in the histories. They are story-telling talents, but they work better on historical characters and events than on imagined ones. For one thing, the American West gave DeVoto a greater story and more colorful people than any he could possibly have invented. There is nobody in his novels who belongs in the same gallery with his Narcissa Whitman, Tamsen Donner, Susan Magoffin, Jim Clyman, or that large, empty figure John Charles Frémont, whom DeVoto calls "Captain Jinks of the Horse Marines."

For another thing, fiction demands a ventriloquist, and DeVoto spoke best in his own voice.

Modern fiction has complexities and subtleties of point of view unknown to history. Even the word *objective* has different meanings in the two arts. In history it means *impartial;* in fiction it means *invisible.* The fictional author can make himself invisible either by being a camera or by burying himself in the subjective consciousness of one of his characters, as Camus buried himself in Mersault in *The Stranger.* We may make what we will of Mersault; Camus does not explain him, he only presents him or rather, permits him to present himself. Internal as that novel is, Camus was correct in calling it an exercise in objectivity.

Whatever the point of view, modern fiction rarely utilizes the old omniscience that used to be the stance of both fiction and history and is still the stance of history. Instead of being present as judge and commentator, the novelist now is barely more than a shadow or a half-heard whisper, what Wayne Booth calls the "suggested author." However the problem of point of view is handled, it is the first thing a man sitting down to write a novel must settle. A historian never has to raise the question. The novelist works tentatively, hesitantly, like a man releasing a slipping clutch on a hill, and sometimes he may share E. B. White's nostalgia for the old Model T, on whose pedal one used to step down with complete positiveness, as he might kick open a door. I am fairly sure that Bernard DeVoto came to history with a certain mental relief, precisely because history still works with the Model T's epicycloidal clutch. DeVoto did not want to be off somewhere like the God of creation, indifferent, paring his fingernails. He was a positive man with positive opinions, and he must have liked the sense that as historian he had no need to hide or disguise either his attitudes or his personal gift of language. He did not, in history have to write down to some undereducated or inarticulate or hysterical character; he could write always up to his own level. Once he knew his facts he could be bold, with a novelist's eye for drama and a historian's godlike assumption that he speaks not merely to posterity, but for it.

It is a question whether he ever fully understood how much more at home he was in history than in fiction: his natural impulse was to curse the historian's trade picturesquely, but the curses must be discounted. In the DeVoto papers in the Stanford University Library, there is a file of correspondence between DeVoto and Garrett Mattingly, his friend and mentor, himself a historian of very great distinction. The two criticized each other's work, bucked one another up, lamented serially and in unison, and read one another's lectures, and in the course of twenty-two years managed to discuss most of the problems of historiography. It is a fascinating file. Two men of very different temperament approach history from opposite ends, both working toward that transformation of fact by the imagination that both thought the highest reach of the historian's art. DeVoto was a man whom Mattingly wholeheartedly and all but uncritically admired; Mattingly was a man on whom DeVoto depended as his historical and scholarly conscience. They made a good team, without rivalry. Mattingly, a Renaissance scholar, pretended to know nothing about the American West; DeVoto, a writer, pretended to know nothing about history, though on occasion he thought historians did not know much about it either.

The pretense of incompetence begins early in the DeVoto letters and is never entirely given up. "I can't ever become a historian," he wrote Mattingly in 1933, "for I hate detail and can't spare the time for original research. I'm a journalist, my boy. Besides, the historians being the only group in America who approve of me, it would be a pity to alienate them as I certainly would if I announced I'd forfeited my present immunity as a mere literary gent. . . ." A historian? Me? But in that same letter he was already outlining the book that later would appear as *The Year of Decision: 1846.*

Both that book and *Across the Wide Missouri,* which followed it, were composed as braided narratives following the actions of groups of characters, a complex epic of disparate people all engaged in a single action, the opening of the West, and all revealed through quotation and paraphrase of their letters and journals. This was the sort of history DeVoto found stimulating; if there are complaints about the muse of history in the letters of that time, they are meant jokingly, and they are matched by explosions of enthusiasm, such as the one that reported his discovery of James Clyman as the "culture hero" he needed for a unifying principle. He would not invent, but how happily he discovered in his materials the dramatic and the symbolic! Halley's comet fell into his lap like a shower of pure gold.

But with *The Course of Empire,* which he began writing in the late 1940's, the agonies of history bore down on him. This book, he wrote Mattingly, "is a different *kind* of stuff from its predecessors and I don't enjoy the dilemma, for if this one is history the other isn't, and who am I?" As Mattingly said to DeVoto's friend and assistant, Helen Everitt, when the book was finished,

> Every historian has to grapple with the problem that any significant action occurs in a frame of space, and that the more significant the action the more it is implicated with other actions, antecedent, contemporary and subsequent. . . .
> Tackling anything like the Lewis and Clark expedition in these terms (something I had no idea Benny meant to do when he started) is a pretty heroic enterprise.

To DeVoto himself, the year before, when DeVoto was nearly frantic with the complexity of what he was trying to do, Mattingly had written encouragement:

> This is a different kind of history from anything you have written so far, but it's been implicit . . . in practically

everything you've ever written, and you'd got to the point where it had to be explicit. For your temperament, or mine for that matter, striding across the centuries, hitting the high spots isn't nearly so satisfactory as concentration on a shorter time span. Hard as it is for anyone to know even a very little about North America in 1846 or Western Europe in 1588, it isn't downright impossible; but nobody can cover a line of development over two or three centuries . . . without feeling oppressed by the weight of his own ignorance. . . .

Oppressed he most certainly was. He lamented his own incapacity:

I am not going to join you any longer in the pretense that I have the kind of mind that can write history . . . I am quite incapable of determining facts, recognizing facts, appraising facts, putting facts into relation to one another, confining myself to facts, guiding myself by facts, or even recording facts. My mind is an instrument superbly designed for inaccuracy. . . .

He lamented the errors of the authorities he wanted to depend on:

I'm getting fed up with historians. Yes, & editors of texts too. I worked two weeks trying to find out why my hero Verendrye thought that the same river flowed both north and south in the same stretch. When I finally followed it back to the original text I found that Mr. Burpee, one of your colleagues, had just inserted a comma.

He lamented the endlessness of historical research:

This was supposed to be about Sacajawea, wasn't it? I figure I can clean up the predecessors of L&C in 30 years more, oh, easy. I figure I can do the empires and the wars in less than 10 years more and the trans-Allegheny U.S., the state of scientific thought, symmetrical geography, the diplomatics and American politics in another 10, and maybe in 5 years I can get Napoleon and La. straightened out. . . . Well, God damn it, twice now you've been able to tell me what book I was writing on the basis of the first draft. . . . You damn well better tell me pretty soon what book I'm working toward now or I'll get buried under it. What's in my mind? . . . What book am I aiming at?

To that blast, Mattingly responded soothingly.

You've just got a light case of *regressus historicus.* I've seen some lulus. Thirty years ago [one of my colleagues] decided that he couldn't write about the 16th century German Sacramentarians without a little background of medieval heresies. Now he despairs of really knowing anything about the Albigenses without exploring the 11th century Bogomils and the 9th century Paulicians, and behind them, he knows, are Yezedees and Manichaeans and dark little twisty passage-ways leading off into Persia and Assyria and Egypt. Mean-while he works away doggedly at the connection between Peter Waldo and the Humiliati, at Catherine and Potarini, half a continent and five hundred years from his starting point, which he has practically forgotten.

Buried in multiplying and proliferating sources, cursing his ignorance and his lack of education ("I can't dig out the back-ground of the background of the background. How the hell do I learn historical geography?") DeVoto yearned for some sort of "Instant History":

Did anybody ever write a history of the Seven Years War, in one volume, that I could keep on my desk for reference and could rely on? If the answer is the *Cambridge Modern History,* be so good as to include a teaspoonful of strychnine with your bibliographical note.

He groaned when Mattingly, supplying bibliography like a thesis director, sent him to *Le Métis Canadien* at the suggestion of his colleague John Brebner.

Please drop in on Brebner and shoot him. *Le Métis Canadien* has 1293 royal octave pages. You know my other historical weakness: I have to read all of a book.

Actually he was a glutton for work—twelve to fifteen hours a day seven days a week—and he was also incomparably lucky, for in Mattingly he had the constant assistance and encouragement of a beautifully trained and learned professional. God send all amateur historians such a friend. He steered DeVoto to the right books, he distinguished between reliable and unreliable authorities, he criticized drafts, he bucked up morale, he wrung out crying towels, he summarized peripheral historical matters that DeVoto wanted to know about, such as the Mesta in Spain and the background of Spanish exploration and settlement in the Southwest. He even, humbly, disparaged his own indispensable usefulness, in order to encourage the literary friend whom he considered more brilliant than himself. To hell, he said, with the self-constituted experts to whom DeVoto thought he must pay attention.

> The function of specialists in the historians' economy is to mine and smelt the ore out of which better men write history. I've done that kind of coolie work for years, and have the callouses on my bottom to prove it. . . .

But if he thought that coolie work was all he was doing for DeVoto, he badly underestimated himself. Every once in a while one of his casual remarks touched DeVoto off like a rocket. One instance will illustrate. On November 1, 1945, DeVoto wrote Mattingly in the same mood with which earlier he had described his discovery of Jim Clyman as the culture hero who in his own person had lived the whole West of his time. Now DeVoto was responding to a remark Mattingly had made a few days earlier.

> "American history," says you, with the confidence of a man who boasts that he knows nothing about it, "American history is History in transition from an Atlantic to a Pacific phase." If you didn't say it in that way, don't revise it now, for that's the way I want it. As I say, there is a literary ethics: I will steal what I need as I need it, but not from my friends. And I think I'll begin my book, or end it, or both, with those great words, like the couriers that are stayed not on the frieze. Do you want to be accredited in the text or in a footnote?

Accreditation was in order, for crystallizing a major theme and for other services, including the sort of literary criticism that Mattingly should not theoretically have been needed for. The novelist as historian should at least know how to write. In the face of his mountain of facts, blown by all the thirty-two winds of confusion, DeVoto lost his confidence even in that aspect of the writing of history, and faced the prospect gloomily.

I still know as little as ever and I'm oppressed by it. But also I'm suddenly oppressed by how much I know, at least how much information I have, and how hard it's going to be to impose form on it and make it readable. I suppose there is a structure; I know it's going to be hell to find it. . . .

Chapter by chapter Mattingly helped him find it, or more often corroborated the fact that he *had* found it. And he bent his ear, perhaps not unwillingly, when DeVoto blew up at the woes of composition. He was writing, DeVoto said,

the dullest broth of watery, uremic, and flatulent prose ever compounded, of which there is not only no end but not even a middle. Middle? hell, there is not even an approach, there is not even a beginning. It takes me thirty thousand words to draw even with where I was when I began them. To begin a chapter is enough to make sure that I will be farther from the end of the book when I finish it—farther by twice as many words and God knows how many years. I run furiously, at the extremity of (waning) strength, and the sweat that pours off me is all words, words, words, words, words by the galley, words by the thousand, words by the dictionary, and I sink forever deeper in them, I don't get any farther forward, I only drift back and disappear under them. And Jesus Christ, what words, shapeless, colorless, without sound or substance or taste or perfume or indeed existence, words of immense viscosity and no energy or luminescence whatsoever, words out of a lawyer's brief or out of a New Critic's essay on Truman Capote or the ghost who writes MacArthur's communiques, words of unbaked dough, of glucose thinned with bilge, words less than a serum and somewhat more than an exudation, and in all the mess and mass of them not a God damned thought. . . . With thirteen million words written or by our lady two score million, we have now accounted for 229 years that do not enter at all into my book and have only forty more years to go, or say an even million words, if in the meantime I can learn something about concentration . . . before we reach the beginning of my book and, with a sigh of infinite satisfaction and a suffusing glow of happy realization that only ten million words lie ahead, take up a blank, virgin sheet of paper and write on the top of it Page One.

Any writer will recognize the symptoms, as Mattingly did. This is a man trying to force shape and eloquence upon a resistant and complex body of historical fact. And doing, as Mattingly pointed out, a great deal better than he admitted. Much of the difficulty of this last volume of the western trilogy arose from the fact that it was much less narrative than the others. The generalizer and synthesizer was constantly called on, the novelist had less chance to shine, and he struggled.

Nevertheless, he retained his fictional license, and wherever he could, in brief brilliant flashes, he rendered the explorations of Mackenzie, Frazer, Thompson, Peter Pond, as story; and he made of the Lewis and Clark expedition a symbolic journey to the end of what Columbus had begun, the full achievement of the Northwest Passage to history's Pacific phase. And he didn't fail to heed, even when his materials were recalcitrant, the advice he had given Mattingly years before in 1938. If there was one thing wrong with Mattingly's writing, he had said then, it was "forgetfulness, or momentary disbelief, that the reader is in there working too. In narrative fewest is best and you don't have to tell everything, for if anyone is with you at all, he is half a yard ahead of you . . . you're probably giving him more than he needs."

Here is the touch not of a recorder but of an artist: being possessed of mountains of material, restrain yourself, don't dump it all on the reader. Let him come climbing eagerly in discovery. And some other advice he had given, touching on the uses of the dramatic:

> I think you lean over a little backward—I think you refuse to let yourself utilize all the emotional possibilities, sometimes, on the unconscious theory that you'd be popularizing if you did. . . . It's almost as if you pulled up at second base because no scholar ought to knock a home run. Whereas for the dignity of scholarship every scholar who can write, which is damned few, ought to write his head off. . . . When you get a scene, play it. I'd even sacrifice all the dispensable detail in order to get room for drama. You know I'm not arguing that you should leave out anything that ought to be in, or that you ought to pump up a scene that hasn't got enough stuff in itself, or in any other way falsify or cheapen the material or the trade. But I am saying that a man who can write as well as you can ought to take advantage of his opportunities.

That is essentially the historical method that both DeVoto and Mattingly aspired to, coming at it from opposite sides. It is a long way from the meticulously pedestrian. It is also as far as possible from the sort of lady-novelist, best-seller history that an editor once urged on Mattingly: "He offers me," Mattingly wrote DeVoto in a rage, "a bewildering choice of subject, from Richard the Lion Hearted to Prince Henry the Navigator ('now there's a great story that's never been told!') to John Hancock, or how about Maria Theresa. He waves away all possible scholarly doubts. 'If you make it part fiction, or just don't put [in] any footnotes,' he says shrewdly, 'nobody but you will know how much you are making up.' "

That editor has since taken up the pen himself and sold hundreds of thousands of copies of doctored and doped "history." In the process he has done harm to the good name of narrative history, and it is perhaps his kind of books which have created prejudice among the professionals. But one does not judge Thucydides by the practice of an untutored local amateur, and one should not judge narrative history by the people who prostitute it. DeVoto and Mattingly, temperamentally different but alike in their distaste for either the tawdry or the dull, have set far sounder examples of how to tell the stories that history provides, without either missing the drama or leaving out the footnotes.

5

The Regional Approach to Literature

GEORGE R. STEWART

*George R. Stewart is a novelist and professor emeritus of English at the
University of California, Berkeley.*

There is a tendency to consider regionalism in literature, and,
more especially, regionalism in the study of literature, as something
recent—a modernistic structure reared upon the wrecked founda-
tions of a slightly older structure called "local color." I should like,
however, to begin my presentation with a quotation from a writer
of a certain antiquity:

> Laudabunt alii claram Rhodon aut Mytilenen
>   aut Epheson bimarisve Corinthi
> Moenia vel Baccho Thebas vel Apolline Delphos
>   insignis aut Thessala Tempe.

And, omitting a few lines, I continue:

> Me nec tam patiens Lacedaemon
> nec tam Larisae percussit campus opimae
>   quam domus Albuneae resonantis
> et praeceps Anio ac Tiburni lucus et uda
>   mobilibus pomaria rivis.

Now, if I may insult you by identifying that quotation, it is from
No. VII of the first book of Horace's *Odes*. And, if I may further
insult you by translating the Latin, I can do so freely:

> Others will praise the famous isle of Rhodes, or Mytilene, or
> Ephesus, or Corinth of the two seas, or Thebes renowned for
> Bacchus, or Delphi for Apollo, or Thessalian Tempe. . . . But
> as for me, not long-enduring Lacedaemon nor the lush

A paper read at the meeting of the National Council of Teachers of English in San Francisco,
November 29, 1948, and published in *College English*, April 1948. Copyright © 1948 by the
National Council of Teachers of English. Reprinted by permission of the publisher and the
author.

meadows of Larissa move me so much as the resounding haunt of Albunea, and the tumbling Anio, the grove of Tibur, and the orchard-fringed banks of her ever changing brooks.

What Horace seems to be doing in this passage is to be writing a manifesto of Roman regionalism. He is saying:

> Our schoolmasters have been drumming it into us Romans for many years about the beauties of Greek poetry, and they have been holding up as ideals those Greek islands and cities. I have no quarrel with their admiration for those places, and I myself grant that Rhodes is famous and Mytilene beautiful and that Corinth and Lacedaemon are great names in poetry. But yet I shall now turn to my little farm in the Sabine hills and celebrate the local scene, which I love in a more intimate way than I ever can those others.

As to what we generally mean by regional literature, there is, I suppose, a loose definition, and there is also a more precise definition. Loosely, we may say that any work of art is regional which has as its background some particular region or seems to spring intimately from the background. But this definition is rather too broad. A novel, for instance, may be located in San Francisco and yet deal with problems of human life which are essentially universal, so that the location in San Francisco becomes only incidental.

There is a rather famous incident in American letters which illustrates this point. Frank Norris, as you remember, had made the statement that of our cities only New York, New Orleans, and San Francisco offered local-color possibilities; and he added, "Fancy a novel about Chicago or Buffalo . . . or Nashville, Tennessee." Whereupon O. Henry wrote his story entitled "A Municipal Report," which is very fine indeed, and is laid in Nashville, Tennessee. And yet, as far as this anecdote goes, O. Henry has not proved his point, and the honors really rest with Norris. For, while "A Municipal Report" is blatantly stated to happen in Nashville, the story is built around the theme of the decayed gentleman and the faithful servant, and it could just as well have happened in Memphis or Mobile or Macon or any other southern city. In fact, with very few changes it could have been located in Milwaukee or in Manchester.

A closer definition of regionalism would require the work of art not only to be nominally located in the region but also to derive actual substance from that location. This substance will be derived from two sources. In the first place, it will come from the natural background—the climate, topography, flora, fauna, etc.—as it affects human life in the region. In the second place, it will come from the particular modes of human society which happen to have been established in the region and to have made it distinctive.

In a certain very real sense we can actually say that all writers have necessarily been regionalists and that most works of literature show at least some regional tone. Those poets of Greece who praised Ephesus and Mytilene were by that very fact regionalists, and that was really the reason for Horace's revolt against them. He was merely asserting the claim of one region as against another. For this reason our approach to the study of almost any author has to be in part regional. Sometimes we forget this, and as a result we lose the flavor of even some of the greatest classics.

The point is of interest enough to call for an example. Let me take an ancient story—one of the most famous of all stories in our Western world—that of the Nativity. As we tell it, the Christ child is adored, on the one hand, by the three men who bear rich gifts of gold, frankincense, and myrrh and are variously called "wise men," "magi," or "kings." By whatever name, they obviously represent the highest level of human society. The child is also adored by the shepherds. Historically considered—that is to say, regionally considered—the shepherds undoubtedly stood for the lowest grade of society, so that in the juxtaposition of the kings and the shepherds we have the high and the low, that is, symbolically, all mankind. In the United States, in spite of our having no kings, we still catch that side of the symbolism, but we generally miss the other. To show why we do is a problem in the regional approach to literature.

To demonstrate, we need go back to medieval England, a great wool-producing country, where many men spent their lives being shepherds. As doubtless also in ancient Palestine, these shepherds were socially of very low rank, and as such we see them represented in the *Second Shepherd's Play*. The first English immigrants to America, therefore, must have brought with them a clear and proper idea of the Nativity story. The eastern part of the United States, however, never developed into a region where great flocks of sheep were kept beneath the care of special workmen called "shepherds." The word "shepherd" thus seems actually to have gone out of current use except in a kind of romantic literary connection. Ordinary people knew it from the Nativity story, perhaps from the tradition of pastoral poetry, and certainly from the Twenty-third Psalm, in which the shepherd is a very important personage indeed.

After a while, however, the Americans entered the western part of their country, which was suitable for the keeping of large flocks under special guardians. By this time apparently the word "shepherd" had become so literary and poetical that it seemed unfitting for these (far from literary or poetical) actual keepers of sheep, and a new word was coined: "sheepherder." The contrast in connotation between "shepherd" and "sheepherder" in the United States, especially in the West, is tremendous. A sheepherder is still what the shepherd once was—the lowest of the low. To tell the Nativity story for a child in Nevada or Montana, we would say that, on the one hand, came the kings and, on the other, the sheepherders.

Now and then things work the other way. I mean, in our western region we come closer to some old masterpiece and catch intimately some flavor which has vanished for those people of England and our eastern states. Take the lines in Fitzgerald's *Rubáiyát:*

> . . . some strip of herbiage strown
> Which just divides the desert from the sown.

One could do a whole dissertation on the word "desert" in its shifting meanings and suggestions. Here I can only point out that to an easterner the passage is merely literary in its reference but that any country boy in California or Arizona is sharply alive to the idea and image of crossing "the line of the ditch" and passing in three steps from green, cultivated acres into full desert.

Or let me take again a biblical story. We are told that Adam and Eve "sewed fig leaves together" for garments. I suppose that to the most grave theologians of Cambridge and Oxford, and of Massachusetts Bay also, the reason for the choice of fig leaves rather than of some other leaves must have been just another mystery of the divine purpose, unless, indeed, they had allegorical interpretations. But any child in Fresno or San Jose would know why they took fig leaves. It was for a very practical reason and one which improves our opinion of the common sense of our first parents. It is merely

that fig leaves are very large. If they had tried to sew together some
olive leaves, which are quite small, that would indeed have
demanded explanation as part of the divine mystery.

Here again we see that all literature is likely to demand a
regional approach in its study. This is because no one—not even
though he takes for himself the study of all mankind—can always
and wholly deny the influence of that place in which he lives. For
even through an ivory tower the wind of the country blows,
bringing perhaps the smell of pine woods or perhaps of new-
plowed land or perhaps of an oil refinery; but still it blows. One of
our poets has expressed this well for the first settlers at Jamestown:

> And those who came were resolved to be Englishmen,
> Gone to the world's end, but English every one,
> And they ate the white corn-kernels, parched in the sun,
> And they knew it not, but they'd not be English again.

> —S. V. BENÉT, *Western Star*

First of all, to make Europeans feel different, there was the great
unbroken forest, so that in our speech we still talk not of "a wood"
but of "the woods," implying that there is no limit. Even after the
forest was cleared, things were not the same as they had been at
the old home. There was a violence to the new country, as
compared with the old—a violence of wild men and beasts, a
violence of summer heat and of the bitter cold of winter.
"Blizzard" was a new word they had to learn along with the thing
itself; and so also "hurricane," "chinook," and "tornado." During
the decades when Elizabethan Englishmen were turning into
eighteenth-century John Bulls, those other Elizabethan Englishmen
who had come to America were in some ways retaining more of the
Elizabethan traits of recklessness and violence and in other ways
developing still different traits. This was partly, of course, because
they were mingling and associating with Frenchmen and
Dutchmen and Indians and Negroes and other peoples, but partly,
also, the regional influences were different.

And we should all, I think, admit that we have changed. Part of
the change results from the passage of time, and that kind of
change we are readiest to admit. But part of the change also results
from change of place. Thus we develop still another regional
dislocation or nonconformity with the older literature, much as we

may deny it. Because of this change of place, from the point of view of Chaucer and Shakespeare, the plant that we call "corn" is not corn; the bird that we call "robin" is not a robin; the fish we call "trout" is not a trout; the animal we call "elk" is not an elk. Something like this, I presume, another of our poets meant when he wrote symbolically:

> Only they speak in the tongue of another country
> There are names in their speech of fruits unknown
>   in these valleys
> Also their gods are carved with the muzzles of jackals
> And their proverbs are proverbs made in a dry place.

> —ARCHIBALD MACLEISH, "Land's End"

Now I think that it is a good thing to try to hold onto the best of the past and the best not only of England but also of all countries. And yet it becomes difficult.

I read to my students those very beautiful lines from the opening of the second book of Chaucer's *Troilus and Criseyde:*

> In May, that moder is of monthes glade,
>   That fresshe floures, blew and white and rede,
> Ben quike again, that wynter dede made,
>   And ful of bawme is fletyng every mede.

The passage means something directly to me because I happen to have spent my boyhood in a region where May was not wholly unlike the May of Chaucer's England. But to my students the passage is wholly literary and lacks immediate emotional appeal. One of my colleagues tells me that he makes it the occasion of a whole hour's lecture on conditions of life in medieval England. Perhaps after that the students can at least understand the passage, but we can doubt still whether it makes much immediate poetic appeal to them, and in any case the rate of exchange—one hour's lecturing for four lines of poetry—is high.

This passage, I suppose, may give trouble also in Houston, in Miami, in Louisville, and in Kansas City. I am not absolutely certain, but I doubt very much whether in any of those cities May can properly be called the "mother of glad months." Quite the contrary, I should guess. In most of California, certainly, May has associations almost the opposite of those it had for Chaucer. It is the time of the death of the year when the hills turn brown, cracks begin to gape in the adobe soil, first forest fires blaze up, and all creatures brace themselves for the long drought which may not be broken until November.

On the other hand, a California poet writes:

> Though the little clouds ran southward still, the quiet
>   autumnal
> Cool of the late September evening
> Seemed promising rain, rain, the change of the year.

>   —ROBINSON JEFFERS, "Autumn Evening"

If you are a Californian, you will not need to have pointed out to you in an hour's lecture that rain comes on a south wind and that late September may bring rain, the end of the summer drought, and the change of the year.

In what I have said I have perhaps wandered too far afield for the practical purposes of this meeting. In concluding, I shall be more specific. I have had some experience in teaching courses in American regional literature. What reasons do I see for their existence?

The first reason is that which has been implicit in all that I have already said, that is, in writings which are the product of his own region (other things being equal) the student finds a quicker and easier and more immediate appeal. There are likely to be many barriers between the ordinary student and the appreciation of literature—the barriers of time, of place, of sophistication, and many others. The regional approach at least gets rid of one of these barriers—that of place.

In the second place, there are emotional—perhaps sentimental—advantages. We remember in MacLeish's *Conquistador* that the old man Bernál Díaz inveighs against the history of Gómara, because Gómara has written merely from literary sources, and so Díaz cries out:

> But I—
> Fought in those battles! These were my own deeds!
> These names he writes of, mouthing them out as a
>   man would
> Names in Herodotus—dead and their wars to read—
> These were my friends: these dead my companions.

The student who reads a regional book cannot say exactly this, but at least he can say it of the places—"I have walked here; I have climbed this pass; I too have seen the little clouds run south in September!" And this also is a valuable aid to breaking down what may too often be called a kind of resistance to good reading.

In the third place, I would rest a case for regional literature upon what I should call a cultivation of an intelligent provincialism. I am aware, of course, that the chief argument against such courses is that they lead to the glorification of provincialism. But, after all, the great majority of people are destined to be, in some sense, provincials—and so why not try to make them good provincials, not provincials by prejudice, but knowing something about their own province for good or for bad, and, therefore, better able to function also as citizens of the world? To make a political analogy, we should all distrust the fundamental political goodness of some person who worked for the United Nations and then neglected to vote in his local elections. So, to speak for myself at least, I find myself distrusting the fundamental cultural goodness of a Californian who moves merely in such company as that of Homer and Dante and Shakespeare, without having read such works as *The Luck of Roaring Camp, The Jumping Frog, Death Valley in '49, Mountaineering in the Sierra Nevadas,* and *The Octopus.*

Eventually, I suppose, all justification of the study of literature must rest upon a belief that it makes the individual a better citizen and a happier person. It seems to me that I have observed instances in which the study of regional literature has achieved this result, when perhaps the study of a more distant literature would not have done so.

I began with Horace's manifesto for regionalism; let me end with Chaucer's. For, we must remember, in Chaucer's time England was only a small province of Catholic Europe, far removed from the cultural capitals of France and Italy. In one of the most charming passages that that great poet ever wrote, though he wrote it in prose, Chaucer addressed "his little sone Lewis" in the prologue to his *Treatise on the Astrolabe.* And since it is in prose I shall modernize:

> This treatise . . . will I show thee under full light rules and naked words in English [for, of course, use of the local language is essential to regionalism]. . . . But nevertheless

suffice to thee these true conclusions in English as well as suffice to these noble Greek clerks these same conclusions in Greek; and to Arabians in Arabic, and to Jews in Hebrew, and to Latin folk in Latin; which Latin folk had them first out of other diverse languages . . . and yet by diverse rules; right as diverse paths lead diverse folk the right way to Rome.

And there let me end, merely pointing out that there are, as in Chaucer's time, many kinds of people and also many different ways of approaching literature. One of these is by way of regionalism.

6

The Historical Novel

A. B. GUTHRIE, JR.

A. B. Guthrie, Jr., is a Montana writer whose best-known novel is The Big Sky.

I'll try to tell you today why some novelists choose to deal with the past. And I'll give my justification for the choice, if justification can be found for literary endeavors that so many people regard so dubiously. The historical novel, as you know, is by reputation a sort of tramp in the parlor of letters—and not altogether through pure prejudice. We historical novelists at times have worked pretty hard for that reputation.

The reasons for this choice of time, of course, differ with writers; no one can answer entirely for the rest of us. So allow for accident. Allow for mercenary speculation. Allow for undifferentiated preference.

An old Kentuckian I've heard about one night found himself at an old-fashioned revival, an old fashioned and, I believe, Methodist testimonial meeting at which the worshipers one by one, got up to tell how they had been led to see the light. Finally all but the old man had testified. The others gathered around him, urging him to speak his piece, too. Finally, and reluctantly, he got to his feet.

"Sistern and Brethern," he said, "I've tried sinnin' and I've tried not sinnin', and I swear to my soul I believe I like sinnin' the best."

So some of us writers of historical novels may just like sinnin' the best.

But beyond what may be called mere idiosyncracy, there must exist considerations that quite a body of us in degree have been influenced by.

I'll get to them presently. First I'd like to clear the ground for a

A talk delivered to the Pacific Northwest History Conference, Helena, Montana, May 1954, published in *Montana: The Magazine of Western History*, Fall 1954. Reprinted by permission of the author.

more general discussion by listing the small and particular, but perhaps decisive, reasons for my own choice.

I write historical novels, historical novels of the West, out of a long-time interest in the westward movement in America. I can't remember when the subject didn't attract me. John Burroughs, the naturalist, said, "I am in love with this world; by my constitution I have nestled lovingly in it. It has been home." I think I can say that I have been and am in love with this West I write about. It has been home, too; home seen the more lovingly and I hope the more clearly because the impassable years lie between us. The years impassable except to imagination, except to devotion. Along the beavered streams of Montana, I hear the old shouts of the fur hunters. On the ridges I can see the Blackfeet passing. An arrowhead found in some dusty buffalo run becomes a chase. An ox yoke becomes a wagon train. An old spur belongs to Andy Adams, the cowboy from Texas. Indian, mountain man, home-seeker, gold-hunter, gunfighter, cow-puncher, cattleman, honyaker—they people this world. They move against the great backdrop of plains and mountains that echo still to shouts and whispers and curses and prayers; to the whines of dry axles, the cries of babies, the boom of a cap and ball. And all of this and all of them are dust; except that they rise from the dust through the magic of what we call daydream in youngsters and imagination in adults. No matter. They are dust and they arise; and, arising, give richness to life.

I suppose I am a sort of antiquarian. Flint and steel interest me more than the everlasting match. I prefer a muzzle-loader to a machine-gun. I can get excited over a wagon train, not much over a Constellation. Kit Carson and Jim Bridger stay in my mind after the boys of the wild blue yonder have left it. I like old cherry more than knotty pine.

So, if I was to write, it was natural that I turn to the West and to its earlier days.

I don't know when I began feeling that justice hadn't been done to the fur hunter of the 1820's and the 1830's, justice not in the sense of idolatry but of truth, of proportion. We have enough creators of idols, who make one admirable quality the sum of the man; not enough honest appraisers who recognize that a part of all heroes is the clay common to all of us. The great men of our folklore are made to appear almost spotless. I don't believe in them. I don't even like them very well. Perfection is something we strive for, but that no one ever attains, thank heavens! What we need to remember, in the reconstruction of heroes, is just that no one ever was perfect. I wanted to show the mountain man—in this first book of mine—for what he was, or what he seemed honestly to me to have been—not the romantic character, the virtuous if unlettered Leatherstocking, but the engaging, uncouth, admirable, odious, thoughtless, resourceful, loyal, sinful, smart, stupid, courageous character that he was and had to be.

It occurred to me, as I worked at the idea, that another universal entered here, the universal of Oscar Wilde and "The Ballad of Reading Gaol." Each man kills the thing he loves. No men ever did it more thoroughly or in a shorter time than the fur hunters of General Ashley and Jed Smith and Jim Bridger. For a short thirty years they knew their paradise—freedom, excitement, adventure, solitude, the cozy satisfaction of planting feet where white feet had not trod before. And then it was all over—beaver trapped out, Indians tamed, buffalo on the wane, lonely trails peopled by home-seekers, the rule of free action supplanted by statutes filed in courthouses. Nothing was left.

All of us, it seems to me, do the same thing, if not so spectacularly or completely, through some evil accident of existence. Not that we are unconscious or wanton. We kill the thing we love because we don't have clean choices and, lacking them, destroy our loves by a sort of attrition until at last, numbed and sullied by necessity, we may wonder what it was we ever loved, or how it was that once we loved it. That is one of the tragedies of the lives we have to lead. We never have the clean choices that our youth and innocence have led us to expect; and not having them, weaken or lose our attachments in the compromises we can't avoid.

Well, in any case, there was a theme here that attracted me. I would write the story of the mountain man.

Finally—and this is both a personal and, I believe, a general reason for the novelist's first resort to history—perhaps my choice was determined, in degree, by the thought that the past was easier to deal with than the contemporary. Here was something ready-made, waiting only to be learned and wrenched into some sort of shape. The use of it, beginning novelists are likely to think until experience teaches them better, will save a lot of wear and tear on the imagination. And it will ease the problem of filling out a manuscript to book length. Lug in history when the mind lags.

Drag it in, boot and heels. Draw on the bric-a-brac, the trappings, the recorded customs, manners, techniques. Such borrowings may not forward the story exactly, but they will be easy. More, they will demonstrate the borrower's familiarity with history. They'll show he's qualified as a novelist because he's a good historian.

What conveniences, what advantages does history offer the novelist? It offers him, to list a small but not unimportant item, the convenience of easy novelty. I believe it was Edmund Gosse who said that the secret of successful narrative was a continual slight novelty. It isn't difficult thus to season a re-creation, not if you know your time and place and people. Employed rightly, the little fact that people of early-day St. Louis used to use bear oil in lieu of lard, heightens and helps to hold the reader's interest. For such a fillip the author of contemporary fiction likelier than not has to invent.

But here, perhaps, is the biggest common reason for history in fiction. History offers perspective. From our present-day vantage point we can assess its significances. We know, or feel we know, its pitch, tone and place in the long stream of experience, whereas we may be confused and baseless in the present. From what point do we approach the present, with what real perception, with what valid assumptions? On-the-spot reporting is subject to amendment, when the thing seen is seen together with the things it blinded us to.

I'm not saying, of course, that the contemporary doesn't offer opportunities for the novelist. Obviously it does, and fiction would be in a sorry state if it didn't. I'm just suspecting, out of my own experience, that many historical novelists doubt their ability to deal with it. I am more at home with the materials when they are dusty.

Against any advantages in the use of history, there are burdens, difficulties, temptations, dangers not found elsewhere. For one thing, the author must know his history—or let me say, he ought to. If he is conscientious, he can't assume, ignore, distort, or falsify. He has to know for other than ethical reasons, too. Someone is sure to catch his errors. The littlest anachronism will excite a howl. Once when I was working long hours to meet a deadline, I was led to use a name that I found in recent but not old literature. The name was Nyack, and the thing named was that small creek in Montana, a tributary of the Flathead. The chances seemed at least a thousand to one that the present name was old. The fur hunters didn't give titles to mountain ranges, peaks, plateaus or stretches of plains, not often at any rate. But they did name the rivers because the rivers were the scenes of their operations. The consequence is that nearly all western-stream names are more than a hundred years old. I took the one chance in a thousand, telling myself, moreover, that the stream was unimportant, except of course to my story, and that such a little matter didn't justify a further search. Maybe it didn't, but the book hadn't been long in print before I received a letter. The writer said it was his impression that Nyack Creek was named at the time the Great Northern railroad was building its line through Montana, a half century after the time of my story. He was right, too. I've always wondered, since he caught me in one mistake, how much confidence he put in the rest of my history.

Perhaps it should be added here that the historical novelist must be prepared for criticism that is itself in error. A midwest book reviewer said *The Big Sky* would have been better if I hadn't employed such modern gangsterism as the phrase "rubbed out." Now "rubbed out," meaning killed, meaning done away with, is old. I do know that it was drawn, probably in the first years of the 19th century, if not earlier, from the Indian sign language. When an Indian wanted to impart the information that a man had been killed, he rubbed the fingers of one hand against the palm of the other. Hence, "rubbed out." So the fact is that today's gangsters aren't modern at all in this case. They borrowed an idiom a hundred and fifty years old. The reviewer, had he wanted to, could have found a more recent but still dusty example. Custer's soldiers, singing "Garry Owen" as they marched to their last rendezvous, boasted that they would rub out the Sioux.

The historical novelist must know his history—which means that in the actual preparation of a book he must spend at least as much time in research as in writing. He must read the prime sources, take adequate notes, arrange the notes so that he can put his hands on them when he wants them. (Sometimes a man gets the feeling that he ought to take notes on his notes.) More than that, his very choice of a subject is usually the result of a long and interested, if unmethodical, reading about the time and place and people with which he expects to deal. The writer of contemporary fiction doesn't encounter such a necessity.

What do I mean when I say the historical novelist must know his history? I mean that he must know not only the broad outlines, the social conflicts, the political, military and economic concerns and consequences of his setting; he must know how men talked, what they wore, with what techniques they fashioned their lives, how they regarded and how they met the questions that still may bother us today. It isn't enough, as one writer has said it is, to describe a carriage as a "handsome" carriage. The conscientious novelist wants, and needs, a more specific and less editorial description. "Handsome" in relation to a carriage could fit many places and almost any time—which is to say that it says nothing.

Even an acquaintance with the sticks and stones of history isn't enough. The fictionist in history must be able to read between the lines of his sources, which, in American literature at least, tend to be restrained, staid, proper, in accordance with an old conviction that a lot of what went to make life wasn't fit for print. He must fill in, synthesize, guess intelligently, for what he's trying to tell about is life as it was lived, not alone as it was reported. I'll draw on my own experience again, not because the example is superior or even necessarily good, but because it is at least mine. When I was experimenting with a story about the Oregon Trail, I began to wonder about the women, the largely unsung heroes of the great movement to the West. I wondered how they felt, what they felt, how they acted. Here was two thousand miles of journey ahead of them, to a land almost unknown, a land of loneliness, of savages, of guessed-at hardships and terrors. A land without doctors or even midwives. I wonder how many men would have gone had they been women. A prairie schooner, jolting remorselessly over plain and mountain, wasn't the ideal spot for nausea, nor a tent nor a sequestered cabin, if they were lucky enough to be in one, the ideal spot for childbirth.

It is in directions like these, I believe; it is in the direction of rounding out life, of seeing it in the whole, that the historical novelist may give real service to history.

I've already indicated another danger. It is the danger of what might be called the unblended record, the undigested mass. The tired author too often is tempted to throw in a tired chunk of history. These chunks constitute a hurdle, or a series of hurdles, that the reader may or may not jump in order to find his hero on the other side. A good historical novel has to be on open highway, with no slows or stops for the road blocks of antiquity. It has to be more than ghosts among the gimcracks. It has to be more than history faintly inhabited by figures. It has to be people, it has to be personalities, set in a time and place subordinate to them. Perhaps the hardest lesson for us historical novelists, as it is also the hardest lesson for any writer of fiction, is that it isn't event that is important; it is human and individual involvement in and response to event.

We come now to the two great problems, the two great questions to which there are no complete answers. There are only fractional answers. There are only answers at best to specific cases. Shall the historical novelist deal with the actual figures of history, with the actual events, or shall he go outside them? If he goes outside, what shall be his limits? If he employs the record, what violences, if any, may he do it? May he invent words for the mouths of corpses, may he have dead limbs acting as live limbs never did, may he amend the facts, extend the annals? May he have a soldier survivor on General George Armstrong Custer's battlefield, as one author did?

My answer is my own, and I suppose a part of it already has been given. I don't like to tinker with the facts. I don't like to assume, no matter if I can't actually be proved wrong, that an actual mouth said something or that an actual body did something that has no support in the record. Liberties like these tend to muddy history, as the little story of George Washington and the cherry tree has muddied history. And they seem to me to be almost acts of disrespect, like disfigurements of headstones. If we use the record —I'm talking of known events, known people, known words—then, ideally at any rate, we must let ourselves be the prisoners of it.

But the position poses still another and difficult question. Things don't happen in the shape of novels, not once in an age. They happen haphazardly or anticlimactically or in contradiction to the demands of literary form, with violence to the rule of rising interest and climax and proportion. Fiction isn't fact; it is the representation of fact, which writers hope is truth; and as representation it requires authorial management of the facts. So how can one have a novel if he sticks absolutely to the record? I guess the answer is he can't.

The alternative remains. At least it seems to remain for me. I haven't had to use the record, in the degree, I mean, that we've been talking about. In writing of the mountain man or the traveler to early Oregon, I didn't have to deal with an actual keelboat trip, an actual party of fur hunters, an actual journey across the plains. I could make up my properties, my adventures and my cast, using the real paraphernalia as models for my own, the real adventures only as suggestions, the real characters as background figures, held within the limits of what I could learn of them. As background, the people of history would help to establish time, place, atmosphere, general situation. Besides, they had at least to be mentioned. How could any reference to Jim Bridger or Jed Smith be omitted in the story of the beaver trade?

It probably doesn't need to be said that even this approach involves commitments to fact. The author has to be true to his period and his place. His people have to talk as people did, dress as people did, employ the techniques that people did. The concerns of real people have to be the concerns of his cast. The big events, the big questions, the big conflicts of the times can't be ignored; they must be reflected in the degree that they would have been had his characters been sure-enough persons.

The field is freer, nevertheless, and I think the novelist working in it may discover profits more important than mere convenience. I think he may find his novel is a better novel, a more illuminating novel, a novel really truer to times and people than if he had chosen to star actual event and individual. I don't know but that even the writer without too great a respect for the record would find that to be true. There are limits even to the violences that may be inflicted on history. The writer in this freer field can point up theme by the manipulation of the details in which theme so often is lost. He can underscore significances because he is the master and not the servant of his materials. And so he can give us a story in the round, a story with a beginning and an ending held together by more than the chance chain of episode.

But it isn't easy, even with invented crews and circumstances, to avoid the amendment or enlargement of fact. That is one of the reasons that I said no answers to the problem were complete answers. Somewhere in your story the man of your mind may collide with the man of history. Somewhere the imagined situation may mix with the real. The man of fact has to speak; the real situation has to be dealt with. So what do you do? Well, I do the best I can. I try to make the man true to character—and I don't let him talk very much. I avoid, if I can, any alteration of situation, even very minor ones. These deviations from the rules I've made for myself don't disprove the rules. The rules are still good. It's just that they're sometimes beyond my reach.

I suppose it can be asked why historical novels should be written at all, aside from the strictly personal and mercenary considerations of the author? The facts of history are there, in histories, for anyone who wants to know them. We know the issues and the events, or we can learn them. And by their recorded actions and utterances we know the men and the kind of men who lived in a given time and place, just as we know a tree by its fruits.

Answers to the questions are several. First, not enough history is being taught, not enough is popularly known. The historical novel, if not a defensible substitute for history, still is better than nothing.

And, even if students were taught enough history, and if adults knew enough, the historical novel, it seems to me, could be justified. This is so if only because the good ones clothe the bones of history with flesh and re-create for us the people, problems, passions, conflicts and social directions that, in nonfiction treatment, remain dust for too many of us. Men aren't known by their actions, or let us say that they don't live and breathe and acquire dimension through a knowledge of them alone. Men must be known through the whys of action, too. Understand a man thoroughly, and you can predict how he'll act. The best of the historical novelists seek to do that—to understand men and to acquaint you with them. Thus their actions become, not accidental or inexplicable, as many actions are, but of a piece with the men themselves. And so actions and men both are real, both persuasive and together illuminative of the record.

At a meeting of historians I hesitate to say what I'm going to, for I am immensely indebted to patient and painstaking men who gathered and put on paper the materials from which I have borrowed. It seems to me, however, that the historical novel may find some support in the unhappy circumstance that so much of history is badly written and hence discouraging to readers. The writers of history, save for half a dozen or so, appear, like other specialists, to be committed to their specialty beyond rightful concern for felicity of expression. To them it is as if facts were all-important and manners of statement trifling and affected, whereas facts without communication are trifling and the indifference to presentation itself affected.

I want to quote here from an excellent leaflet written by Samuel Eliot Morison, the Harvard historian, or, rather, to quote quotations he uses. The leaflet is entitled, "History as a Literary Art." The first quotation is an excerpt from an address made by Theodore Roosevelt before the American Historical Association in 1912. It says of the historian:

"He must ever remember that while the worst offense of which he can be guilty is to write vividly and inaccurately, yet that unless he writes vividly he cannot write truthfully; for no amount of dull, painstaking detail will sum up the whole truth unless the genius is there to paint the truth."

The second expression is from the writings of the late A. N. Whitehead:

"The sense for style . . . is an aesthetic sense, based on admiration for the direct attainment of a foreseen end, simply and without waste. Style in art, style in literature, style in science, style in logic, style in practical execution, have fundamentally the same aesthetic qualities, namely attainment and restraint. The love of a subject in itself and for itself, where it is not the sleepy pleasure of pacing a mental quarterdeck, is the love of style as manifested in that study.

"Style, in its finest sense, is the last acquirement of the educated mind; it is also the most useful. It pervades the whole being. . . . Style is the ultimate morality of mind."

If the historical novel needs a further, and moral, justification, the justification can be found, and in it also a support for the position that not enough history is taught or known. I'm speaking particularly, though not exclusively, of the American historical novel. I believe all of us become better citizens, better and richer human beings, through a familiarity with the dreams and deeds of the men and women who went before us in this adventure that we call the United States of America. I think we cannot appreciate freedom, opportunity, progress, convenience, or obligation, without this understanding of spent hope and sweat and blood and treasure. And I'm afraid most of us don't understand.

I suppose I don't need to mention the pleasures to be found in history; of the day-by-day rewards of an interest in it, of the riches that a knowledge of the past brings to the now, of the feeling of personal position, of oneness with all time that that knowledge gives us. Ben Ames Williams once wrote, "There is no past; the past is now." Only those who have lived the old years through the facts of history and the magic of the imagination can know what he meant.

7

The Novelist and His Background

VARDIS FISHER

Vardis Fisher (1895–1968) was a prolific novelist considered one of America's foremost regional writers.

When it was suggested that I should take as my topic this evening "The Novelist and His Background" I felt dismay, even though it may be supposed that serious writers—of whom, alas, I pretend to be one—know something about the subject. Mention of "serious" writers usually recalls for me the story of that tedious congressman who, after wearying his colleagues with a long-winded speech, turned to Henry Clay and said, "You, sir, speak for the present generation but I speak for posterity." Henry Clay, you will remember, said to him, "You seem resolved to speak until the arrival of your audience." All serious writers like to believe, with the congressman, that they speak for posterity; but as we approach old age we begin to understand that we do very well indeed if we speak for ourselves.

I felt dismay at the thought of talking to this group because I am not in any special sense of that word a folklorist. Still, any writer, I suppose, is a folklorist, or any artist of any kind. My dictionary says that folklore is the customs and beliefs of a people or a study of them. In that sense folklore is as broad as human life itself, and a novelist's materials are surely a part of it. In a narrower sense folklore is myth. Myth, any myth, it has been said, is an effort to explain a custom or belief whose origins have been forgotten, or, more likely, were never known. Myth, it may be, is the more spacious formula in which the lore is contained, and myth, I understand after so many years, is the chief thing in a novelist's background.

I do not know how well this matter is understood by people in general. Many years ago when I was a college teacher I was called on the carpet by an angry president, who was tired of hearing complaints about me from parents, alumni, and the board of regents. Pacing back and forth, while wondering whether to fire me or reform me, he suddenly turned and asked, "Fisher, what in the devil do economics, sociology, psychology, and all these things have to do with courses in writing?" If a university president can be so limited in his grasp we hardly dare suppose that there is much comprehension of the way folklore and myth and their wealth of symbols fill and overflow our lives.

In his book on Thomas Wolfe, Mr. Herbert Muller says that Wolfe tried to create the American myth. That statement startled me. Recently, when looking over the first issue of the Denver Faulkner Studies, I was again startled, because I found this author called an epic mythmaker. How, asked the critic, is one to understand Faulkner the mythmaker? It seems to me that here we have confused thinking. No man creates a myth. All myth is a product of the folk mind. It may be true that Wolfe was trying to represent what he conceived to be the American myth; and it may be that Faulkner is trying to search out the substance and color of ancient myth in the American South. But an effort to perceive in what way myth shapes and determines life today is quite different from creating the myth itself.

Freud, toward whom in some quarters it is now the fashion to be indulgent, thought that myth "corresponds to the displaced residues of wish fantasies of entire nations." Otto Rank conceived of myth as an intermediate between collective dreams and collective poems. As the dream draws off the subconscious repressed emotion, so does the myth, creating for itself a "collective symptom for taking up all repressed emotion." Which, in both Freud and Rank, is another way of saying that if our reach does not exceed our grasp, what's a heaven for? It is another way of saying that emotion will create for human yearning those goals which mind cannot establish as fact. For according to Stucken, all myths are creation myths.

For Mr. Muller myth is "not a way of disguising or evading the shocking facts of life but a way of ordering and accepting them." In accepting the shocking facts they are, of course, disguised. Muller goes so far as to believe that all literature, philosophy, religion, yes, and even science is mythology. It would be a great comfort at the moment to know that the atom bomb is a myth. Thomas Mann thinks that the mythical is "the pious formula into which life flows when it reproduces its traits out of the unconscious." But I see no reason why the formula need be pious, unless Mr. Mann intended to imply that the creative act is unrelieved by irony and untouched by doubt.

All these definitions we need not press too far. It may be that we do not quite know what myth is, for the reason that we have not been able satisfactorily to explore the subconscious mind. The mystic, who depends so much more on that mind than most of us, or who in any case makes fuller use of it, is still a riddle. Freud admitted that research in the concepts of folk psychology—that is, myths, sagas, and fairy stories—had not by any means been concluded; and though research has revealed much since his death we still walk in the dark with dim lanterns.

We can, of course, observe mythmaking all around us. We can, that is, observe the creation of legend, which myth absorbs. In 1922 Professor James Weber Linn said to a group of us at the University of Chicago, "I felt like a lion in a den of Daniels." He claimed that witticism as his own, though it was old before he was born. In the *Reader's Digest* for March, 1950, Herbert Corey solemnly attributes the witticism to Willmot Lewis, and gravely informs us that since Lewis first said it in 1931—that is, nine years after Linn said it—it had enlivened the orations of hundreds of speakers. In such manner the folk mind works in the creation of its heroes. In some such manner, we may assume, myth is born.

Or we may take as another instance the way certain votaries are striving to bring their cult-gods to apotheosis—as Malcolm Cowley and John O'Hara with Ernest Hemingway, or a group of disciples with W. H. Auden, or such magazines as *Life* with such persons as Rita Hayworth, who not so long ago was elevated to the throne of Venus—and hastily dethroned after she took up with an Eastern prince. These people are only doing for their heroes what others are doing for F. D. Roosevelt, or for Tito, or for Stalin, or for various other demigods, whose stature rises in legend all around us, and whose embellishments will coalesce eventually to make the myth, which will become a part of biographies yet to be written.

As I see it, the chief task of the novelist is sufficiently to liberate himself from his background to be able to see it in some kind of perspective. That he was unable to do so up to the time of his death was the tragedy of Thomas Wolfe. He was so enmeshed, so suffocated, so much the captive of all the forces that had made him that he actually could place himself, as in the fourth chapter of *Look Homeward, Angel,* as a swaddled babe, still unable either to talk or walk, in the position of a sardonic and matured adult. In varying degrees we are all guilty; and we are guilty because the lore and myths of our world enfold and imprison us, embellishing our meaning and glorifying our ego. We have in some manner to break free, without on the one hand losing touch with the stuff that made us, without on the other mistaking our self-protective illusions for truth. And the threat of a deeper and deeper schizophrenia broods over the struggle.

A novelist's background, it seems to me, is to be found less in the physical accidents of his life—in parents, neighbors, and geography —than in the past which produced the child. Many years ago a novelist, Budd Schulberg, published a story called *What Makes Sammy Run.* Sammy was a Hollywood heel, and in an effort to understand what made him a heel Schulberg went back to Sammy's childhood. But he never found out what made Sammy run, any more than in a later effort he found out what made Fitzgerald run. I had just read this novel when I said to my friend Professor Don MacRae that it would be interesting to do the same job for some college professor—not that I intended to imply that all, or even most, college professors are heels. MacRae almost at once set himself to the task. The result was his Houghton Mifflin Fellowship novel, *Dwight Craig.* But I do not feel that MacRae was able to tell us what made Dwight Craig run. Some of you may be aware that I once exhaustively explored a man's childhood, in the hope of explaining how he came to be what he was. I also was unsuccessful, and the sense of my failure grows greater with the years.

Those who attempt to find the man in the child are unsuccessful because the man is not there. The man is in all the centuries of our past history. One of Faulkner's critics says that in a Faulkner story everything has been said that it is necessary to say about the part of today that yesterday is. How wonderful if that were true! For if that were true we could now say what makes Sammy run. It would mean that we could talk quite precisely about the novelist and his background. In the midway of this our mortal life, wrote Dante, I found myself in a dark wood, astray. It would mean that we had come out of that dark wood. No man knows, says a line of great poetry, through what wild centuries roves back the rose. It would mean that we could understand the rose back to its beginning. But in plain truth we do not. Not even Faulkner, who so long and faithfully has explored these matters, knows that. Understanding what it is necessary to say about the part of today that yesterday is is exactly the novelist's task. And it is a task that still defeats us.

More than twenty years ago I realized that I had not been able to explain the man in terms of the child. I realized that the author of *The Red and the Black*, great modern that he was, and so remorseless in searching out the truth, had not explained Julien. I fell upon such a fit of depression—in psychological jargon, upon such a frustration of egoistic striving—that I must have been in the condition of the man who, despairing of his sanity, went to see a psychiatrist. What you need, the psychiatrist said to him, is to get out of yourself and away from yourself. The great comedian Grimaldi is in town; go hear him and laugh and forget your trouble. And the poor miserable wretch replied, "Great God, *I* am Grimaldi!"

I was in the kind of funk when a sense of utter futility closes like a shutter on the mind. After some months of despair, which, I am afraid, was wholly devoid of the saving grace of irony, I came to the conclusion that to explain what makes Sammy and Professor Craig and all the rest of us run we must go to the past—which means, simply, that we must explore and try to understand the folk mind, and the myths and symbols it has produced. For an exploration of that vast field one lifetime would never be enough. It is not only that we haven't the time; it is also that we know too little about the marvelous variety and the amazing richness of the symbols which the folk mind has evolved, and which still shape and direct all of us in ways that we never suspect. All the savagery of the past, said the great James George Frazer, lies so close to our surface that it constitutes a standing menace to us and to our civilization. Proof of that we would seem to have had in abundance in our lifetime.

Perhaps without impropriety I may tell you that in the past twenty-five years I have read many hundreds of learned volumes about the past, in those fields most closely related to the novelist's background. If I had the time and the eyes to read another twenty-five years I think I should be right where Grimaldi was when he sought help. I have learned a few things about the evolution of myth; I have stood aghast before the thousands of symbols whose meanings are now a matter of record; but chiefly I have merely opened a window on a tremendous vista which I shall have neither the time nor the mind to penetrate.

I may then be pardoned a touch of annoyance when I read that in a Faulkner story everything about the past has been revealed which is today relevant to the present. Mr. Faulkner, I am sure, must have been amused if he read that statement. He also has been exploring myth and symbol in his effort to understand the American South; and with an ingenuity which no other contemporary writer seems to possess he has been manifesting the past in the present. We must gladly accord recognition to the magnificence of his effort, but we need not be persuaded that he has done more than to search the superficial depths. Another Faulkner critic, for instance, has said that one of his stories may be compared to the transition from the pagan to the Christian era. I do not know if Faulkner so intended it, but there was of course no such transition. Nineteen centuries of Christianity have done no more than to elaborate on and in some instances to refine a great many pagan myths. I raise this point only to suggest that the knowledge of the best of us is still so inadequate that in almost no matter can we be sure that we do not err.

I have stated it as my view that the principal part of a writer's background is the myths that have shaped him. There is a luminous statement in Harold Bayley's brilliant two-volume work, *The Lost Language of Symbolism:* "Little or no distinction can be drawn between classic myth and popular fairy-tale: myth was obviously once fairy-tale, and what is often supposed to be mere fairy-tale proves in many instances to be unsuspected theology." This field is so vast that we have time to look at only one instance. The principal myth of the Western world is not God but what we call the Christ; that is, the myth, found among all ancient peoples, of the deliverer, the savior, and, among all but Jews, the sacrificial offering on the fructifying tree. The wealth of folklore, drawn from so many sources, that went into the making of this symbol is one of the marvels of human history. The tenacity with which the Western world has clung to this symbol establishes its depth in human yearning.

From a great many I choose this myth-symbol, hoping with it to suggest the scope of our problem, as well as its difficulties. We are all aware of that need in mankind for heroes, which Carlyle expressed so well. Heroes we possibly must always have, of some sort, which means only symbols to which we aspire—or if we do not aspire, being too indolent, symbols that serve as points of reference and as moral and spiritual anchors. When hero worship, so strong in the Greeks, was combined with the sacrificial scapegoat, which also was commonplace in the folklore of the ancient world, mankind got its symbol of the savior—and in the process brought women to that degraded level which comprises the most repulsive chapter in human history. We must understand the myth and its sources before we can understand the modern Western woman—or even, I might add, the sensational appeal of Mickey Spillane.

Today, Professor Richard W. Boynton has said in a recent book, we are beyond mythology, or should be. Possibly we should be but we certainly are not. It is not clear that we should be, for the reason that myth has always been the vehicle for what, in any generation, passes for truth. In regard to the Christ symbol, see what form it is taking today! We all know that the Christian churches are fighting for their life. We all know that there is a spiritual force abroad in the world that passes loosely under the name of communism. We all know that this force has had tremendous appeal to a great number of intellectuals; and though I have steadily resisted it, and for seventeen years have been publicly speaking out against it, I was forced to face some unpleasant realities before I turned away from that dark wood. That so many have been, or are now being, disillusioned in this spiritual force is of no interest to us this evening, save as we must wonder what direction the myth will now take.

For the thing called communism—it is not, of course, communism at all—is, as I make it out, a revival on the one hand of ancient emperor worship, which so well served the Caesars, and on the other an invasion, for its dupes if not for its exploiters, of the huge spiritual vacuum being left by the slow withdrawal of Christianity. Professor Boynton thinks that the Christian churches should scrap their antiquated dogmas and replace them with a religion of human values. In short, he would abandon the myth. But myth will not be abandoned, and the hunger for heroes will not be put aside.

What we have then, as I see it, is a return to unabashed hero worship, during this fateful time when an immanent and personal deity is being dethroned. Many people call that godlessness, but very possibly it is not that at all. It can hardly be that as long as the

myth lives in its full vigor. And that today it is in full vigor is
proved by the obvious facts, not only that so many tend to deify
their political leaders, including the late Mr. Roosevelt, but also
that a cradle-to-the-grave security, which the political messiahs
promise, is taking the place of the older belief in a life after death.
In short, the political messiah is replacing the ecclesiastic, and the
"emergency" is replacing hell.

We are today witnesses to this shift in the direction and purpose
of an ancient myth. All things are yours, Paul told the simple folk
who were the early Christians. Under the Christian myth all things
were theirs in a life to come, in which inequities would be no more
and wrongs would be redressed. As Professor Shotwell has said,
"There is no more momentous revolution in the history of thought
than this, in which the achievements of thinkers and workers, of
artists, philosophers, poets and statesmen, were given up for the
revelation of prophets and a gospel of worldly renunciation." That
gospel of worldly renunciation, the reward of which is greater
glories in another life, has been the very heart of the Christian
myth.

Our conflict today is between that gospel, now struggling to
survive, and in the opinion of some doomed to extinction, and the
gospel of the blessed and abundant life here and now. The myth has
veered but it is the same myth. God, again as remote and lost as
that symbol was in the time of Jesus, when the symbol of his son
came down to restore the divine intimacy, now finds his attributes
taken from the ecclesiastic and invested in the politician. It is
tempting to speculate on the development of the myth in the years
ahead; to inquire how long it will survive and what purpose it will
serve; and to ask whether disillusionment in the myth's new form
will be greater than in its old. All that lies beyond us tonight, but
we should note in passing that certain eminent writers, who loathe
the form the myth is taking, have fled the scene and sought a haven
in a moribund church. Mr. T. S. Eliot has said that a rational
civilization will never work; to which, I should think, it is enough
to retort that we can never know until we try it.

Now all this is surely part of a writer's background in a time of
stress and change. It may well be that we apprehend only dimly, if
at all. Novelists of a later age—if the novel as an art form survives,
which is doubtful—will understand far better than we what makes
Sammy run. Today, those striving to understand are at least able to

see, in broad if dim perspective, the outlines of some of the ancient forces which shape us. There are many important myths an exploration of which might well constitute the highest form of intellectual adventure. Sometimes, it is true, we weary in this struggle to understand; and though we may not walk out into the sea, as Virginia Woolf did, or jump off a ship into dark void, as Hart Crane did, we do feel the need to shut out the past which presses with such intolerable insistence upon the present.

In such moments we feel as William James felt about his guests. "Are we never," he impatiently asked his wife Alice, "are we never to have an evening alone? Must I see people every night?" And his faithful wife replied, "I shall see that nobody bothers you this evening." But at the first sound of the doorbell William was there, behind his wife, exclaiming with delight, "Come in! Come right in!" And so it is with us, caught between these persistent guests from the past, whose presence wearies us, and the need to press on and reestablish our kinship with all things.

I have mentioned only one myth among many that are a part of the novelist's background and of the background of all of us. It has been said that all fiction is autobiographical, and that of course is true. Of autobiography, the Professor Boynton alluded to says it "may be somewhat cynically described as the art of informing the world in print what you wish you had been, instead of giving it a portrait of what your enemies and hostile critics said you were." But our hostile critics usually manage to have their say. It is true, nevertheless, that not much fiction, past or present, can stand the scrutiny of enlightened minds. To build it strong and true enough to stand that scrutiny becomes more and more the duty imposed upon us. It was the great achievement of the author of *The Red and the Black*, which a critic as eminent as Taine read a great many times, that he wrote strong and true for his day; and though his contemporaries rejected him we are now proud to acknowledge his worth. That worth lay chiefly, of course, in his great moral courage, and in his intuitive anticipation of certain psychological truths that are now commonplaces.

I might have talked to you of more immediate matters in a novelist's background—of the clues which he must try to find—the clues to his nature and problems. But those clues, it seems to me, all lead back to more remote times, whether they be clues to his emotional hermaphroditism or to his schizophrenia or to the queer symbols in his dreams. They are clues that go back to Job's question, and to Pilate's, both of which remain unanswered. They are clues that go back to the ages, out of which came the stuff that makes the modern child. We have gained so much in knowledge while losing so much out of memory. I am fond of Jean Paul's profound observation that language is a dictionary of faded metaphors. How true that is, any standard work on ancient symbolism will reveal. Which of us, asked Edward Carpenter, has ever seen a tree? None of us has. For ancient peoples a tree was a house of God, a phallic symbol, a miracle standing in the earth-womb, an act of divine creation, a living, breathing thing with speech, powers, and spirit. If we cannot see a tree we have gone a long way from the more intuitive wisdom of the ancients. We must suspect that a great deal remains to be refound and a great deal to unlearn before we see Shelley plain. "All I have written and published," said the greatest of the German poets, "are but fragments of a confession." We have only fragments still.

But as we explore, as we become more familiar with the knowledge which thousands of obscure scholars have put before us; as we understand with Joubert that a man of imagination without learning has wings but no feet; as we make knowledge serve our intuitive insights, we shall add more and more to the great confession which is the history of the human race. We shall lose our self-protective illusions; we shall have to abandon one comforting myth after another; but we need not lose the deep truth which Emerson saw:

> 'Tis not in the high stars alone,
> Nor in the redbreast's mellow tone,
> But in the mud and scum of things,
> There always, always something sings!

8

The Novel in the American West

JOHN R. MILTON

John R. Milton, editor of the South Dakota Review, *is an important critic and scholar of western literature.*

In some respects it should be easier to talk about the Western novel to historians than to professors of literature. The former will at least react sympathetically to the subject matter of many western novels: the cowboy, the mountain man, the military scout or cavalry man, the Indian, and the historical events in which these people played a part. The literature professor wants to know whether the western novel is literary. More than that, perhaps, he has already decided that the western novel is not literary, and to prove it he sets Zane Grey beside William Faulkner, forgetting that Faulkner too was a kind of westerner in some of his concerns. In any case, we need not labor to make the point that the western novel is, and has been, in critical disrepute. Partly for this reason, some western novelists do not want to be called western: Harvey Fergusson quotes the Virginian—"When you call me that, *smile!*" And Paul Horgan feels much the same way. It is true that these men have written novels whose subject matter was non-western. But it is equally true that their best writing has been done with western materials. They are simply reluctant to be wholly identified with a region which in turn has been wholly identified with what we loosely call "the western."

We all know that in the terminology of the professor of literature there are no such labels as "easterns" or "southerns" to match "westerns." We do, however, speak of an eastern novel or a southern novel; that is, we recognize regional distinctions but we are less inclined to pay attention to the eastern-ness or the

A paper presented at the Western History Association Conference, Oklahoma City, October 1964, and published in the *South Dakota Review* 2, no. 1 (Autumn 1964). Reprinted by permission of the author and the *South Dakota Review.*

southern-ness of a novel than we are to its western-ness. The same is true of television. A story which portrays the man in the grey flannel suit on Madison Avenue is not called an eastern or a New Yorker; but a story which centers on a man from Laramie is inevitably a western. There are several reasons for this distinction. The West as a region is, of course, newer than the East or South in terms of established literary and European-cultural traditions. A novel written by a native westerner is still viewed with some curiosity and perhaps mild condescension by the New York critics, as though it had been created by a talented cow much like the chimpanzees which have been painting pictures recently. But more important than this is the stigma attached to the formula novel —the Wild West romance, the cowboy saga, or the cavalry-Indian adventure. We are all too familiar with this story as we have seen it on television. We know, too, of the curious development of the "adult Western," and the sporadic attempts to debunk the myths of the Old West. Some of these myths need debunking, and some do not. The degree to which each western novelist gives serious thought to this matter of myth determines in part his place in the hierarchy of the literary West.

At the risk of over-simplifying a complex matter, let us put western novelists in three groups. At the very least this will give us a point of departure. All western writers maintain some kind of defensive attitude toward eastern publishers, but this collective concern is not enough to make them brothers. Beneath the surface, if we dig, we can see a caste system operating in the West. The so-called upper-crust consists more or less of Walter Van Tilburg Clark, Vardis Fisher, Harvey Fergusson, Frank Waters, Frederick Manfred, and Paul Horgan. Even here we run into difficulties, because Fergusson and Horgan have written eastern novels, and Manfred began his career as a midlander. The group is not a mutual admiration society, although Clark and Fisher are generally ceded the top positions. The second group is a complex one, including major writers who are not convincingly western, good writers who have not produced a large body of work, writers who have moved around just enough to escape some of the regional emphases, and competent novelists who have on occasion nodded in friendly fashion toward popular success. In this last point we see one of the functions of the caste system: it is understood by those "in the know" that a good and honest western writer must be something of a mountain man himself, independent in thought and action, shunning the easy success which his talent could bring him if he bowed slightly to the wishes of the eastern publishers. For this reason, even such a fine writer as Paul Horgan is suspect, although I insist on his position in the first group.

The second group, however, would include at least the following: Wallace Stegner, A. B. Guthrie, Jr., Wright Morris, Tom Lea, Willa Cather, Edward Loomis, Jack Schaefer, Forrester Blake, Conrad Richter, Oliver La Farge, William Eastlake, John Steinbeck, Frank Norris, William Goyen, and Mary Austin—strange bed-fellows. Stegner's novel, *The Big Rock Candy Mountain*, has been rated by Frederick Manfred as one of the twenty best American novels, western or not. I will agree, as long as I do not have to name the other nineteen. *Wolf Willow*, Stegner's most recent book, is a masterful evocation of the northern plains, certainly one of the finest books ever written by an American. Because it is neither a novel nor strictly speaking an exposition or an autobiography, reviewers have not always known what to do with it, and this should please the mavericks. Yet, Stegner publishes often in the slick magazines as an authority on the West, and so displeases his brethren. Guthrie's three novels—*The Big Sky, The Way West,* and *These Thousand Hills*—are highly competent re-creations of the West as it once was. They contain some of the most sensitive and perceptive descriptions of the land in western literature. But they lack originality in many respects, and, with their subsequent movie versions, they proved tremendously popular, as though Guthrie had written them toward that end. Wright Morris flits in and out of Nebraska and is difficult to classify, although his *Ceremony in Lone Tree* must be given serious consideration. Tom Lea *(The Wonderful Country)* is not a big producer, nor is Forrester Blake, else these men would move up in the hierarchy. Blake wrote two excellent novels of the mountain man some years ago—*Johnny Christmas* and *Wilderness Passage* —then retreated to the classroom until his recent book, *The Franciscan*. Willa Cather has achieved a national reputation, and is remembered for two Nebraska novels and *Death Comes for the Archbishop*. But one asks whether her farm novels are not midwestern rather than western, and whether, as Mary Austin has suggested, Miss Cather really knew enough about New Mexico to be considered a westerner. Edward Loomis shows great promise,

especially in *Heroic Love* and *The Hunter Deep in Summer,* but he
has not yet produced the major work which will make assessment
more meaningful. Jack Schaefer stops short of greatness, but not by
much. His *Shane* stands as the classic treatment of one of the
formula stories—the mysterious stranger riding into a town beset
with evil, ridding it of its evil, and riding off into the sunset.
Schaefer's most recent novel, *Monte Walsh,* will also become a
classic in time. It strips the myth and the mist from the cowboy and
shows him plausibly, authentically, and excitingly, with much
understanding, insight, and humor. Conrad Richter is, I think, a
major and neglected American novelist who has suffered critically
because his work is associated with the frontier and yet does not
seem bound to it. *The Sea of Grass,* although a slight novel,
portrayed the pioneer rancher in opposition to the encroaching
farmer so well that it seems silly for anyone else to attempt the
same theme. More recently, *The Lady* also uses western materials,
but Richter remains best-known for his Ohio trilogy. La Farge
upsets me because I respect his knowledge of the Southwest and I
want to admire his books, but I prefer the short fiction to the
novels. His *Laughing Boy* seems to be highly respected, and yet it is
so full of flaws that it is highly susceptible to parody. La Farge's
intentions were honest and worthwhile, but he did not succeed
completely in fulfilling them. William Eastlake also writes of the
Southwest in *The Bronc People* and *Portrait of an Artist with
Twenty-Six Horses.* These novels are imaginative and strong,
treating the Indian with a compassion desentimentalized through
humor. However, Eastlake's imaginative powers often lead him
into fantasy which, when not properly handled, is distracting.
William Goyen, of Texas, has quietly gathered a small group of
admirers and will soon have to be recognized critically. Steinbeck,
too, must be considered seriously even though the critic-professors
seem to have resented his Nobel Prize. At the very least, *The
Grapes of Wrath* must be read in relation to the westward
movement, and *East of Eden* will one day be seen as a major
western novel. Frank Norris, usually associated with the naturalists,
was deeply interested in the course of empire and in the forces of
the land as well as the encroachment of the city. *The Octopus* is a
kind of compendium of western problems, both social and literary.
Mary Austin, considered by some to be the queen of western

writers, is indeed a writer of major importance; but, her best book is *The Land of Little Rain,* not a novel.

The third group, containing many levels of competence and literary worth, has perhaps 100 writers who have turned out thousands of novels, largely in paperback. These are the writers who have made considerable use of the romance, adventure, excitement, nostalgia, and exoticism of the Old West and who usually follow the established formulas closely with particular attention to the cowboy. Some of these are hack-writers, with no further pretensions; others occasionally rise above mediocrity and give us something worth reading. All, however, are part of the phenomenon known as the "western" and must be recognized for what they are. Some of the names are fairly well known: Zane Grey, Luke Short, Eugene Manlove Rhodes, Ernest Haycox, Wayne Overholser, Clay Fisher, Frank Gruber, William MacCloud Raine, Frank Bonham, Louis L'Amour, Frank O'Rourke, Max Brand, and the man who is said to have started it all, Owen Wister. The sad thing is that most of the novelists in this group are capable of better writing than they have usually exhibited. In part, of course, this is simply proof that talent will often submit to commercialism. Rhodes, Wister, and Haycox all have admirers who will defend them on literary grounds as well as historical; but most of the others are old pros who have glutted the market, some of them writing under several names as though in admission of the guilt of over-indulgence. Frederick Faust wrote as Max Brand, Evan Evans, and Peter Dawson—at least. Henry Allen does one kind of novel as Clay Fisher and another as Will Henry. Louis L'Amour, in addition to "his own" novels, carries on the Hopalong Cassidy series under the name of Tex Burns. Harry Sinclair Drago uses his own name in addition to Will Ermine, Bliss Lomax, and Joseph Wayne, giving him the dubious pleasure of being four men rather than one. Only in the formula "western" does one find pseudonymity carried to such length, and if it is not just a method of confounding the tax collector it must surely reveal the commercial attitude which controls this kind of novel.

The three groupings I have made are not entirely defensible, nor are the categories I wish to suggest as a temporary method of breaking down the term "western novel." What the reading public refers to as the "western" is only the formula novel, usually with the cowboy as subject. The formula has also been applied to other materials: the mountain man, the Indian, the cavalry trooper, the settler, the Mormon, the railroad builder, the scout, and so on. If, however, the western novelist takes his work seriously, both in research and composition, and avoids the easy formulas, he is doing for the American West what any good historical novelist has done elsewhere in the United States or in Europe. And so I would like to establish a special place for the historical novel. Finally, we have novels which are semi-historical, in which the author has a pertinent theme going beyond the mere historical facts; we have novels with a contemporary setting in the West, in which the region receives various degrees of emphasis; and we have marginal novels, such as Manfred's *Morning Red,* whose action takes place on the fringes of the Great Plains and Rocky Mountain area, but whose spirit is western. These I call, simply, the western regional novel, for lack of a better term. Again, I think, we have seen the difficulties of laboring under the single term, western novel, for the fiction which is produced in, by, or about the American West. As in any other region, we are confronted with good writing and bad, and with such a variety of intentions, approaches, and subjects that it is unfair to apply a single label indicating little more than an area designation. It just happens that the popularity of one kind of western novel set a pattern from which we are still trying to break away. I am not sure of the precise origins of this pattern, but I am willing to hazard some guesses.

The exploitation of western material for the benefit of naive and awe-struck eastern readers may have begun by accident in James Fenimore Cooper, but it reached a professional level in Bret Harte. Cooper used the image of Daniel Boone, a kind of national frontier hero, to point up the dilemma arising from the confrontation between civilization and the wilderness. To Cooper's credit, he remained stuck with his dilemma, not providing easy answers to sticky questions. Harte, on the other hand, seemed to show that the evils of society could be cured with a breath of fresh and pure western air. We may well believe him, those of us who live in the West, but we must still deplore the artificiality and the ease with which he presented the problem, and the appeal to the exotic qualities of the West with little reference to complicating factors.

Pure adventure and escapism, with emphasis upon thrills and great deeds, became a staple in the dime novels, given considerable

impetus by the fame of William Cody in his role as Buffalo Bill.
The Daniel Boone image moved a little farther west. At the turn of
the century the frontier had closed, but yet another image—that of
Teddy Roosevelt—inspired he-man fiction, and the bestsellers of
Kipling were easily made over into American novels with the
cowboy replacing the British Colonial soldier. The major era of the
cowboy had just ended around 1900, and it was no trick to take him
off his horse and put him into books; he was there, unemployed and
available, and he became a hero. At first, however, he was not the
hard-riding, straight-shooting superman which he grew up to be. As
the Virginian he talked himself out of trouble, rather than shooting
his opponent, until he finally ran out of arguments near the end of
the novel and was forced to kill Trampas. He spent a great deal of
his time pursuing a young lady, whereas we all know that the
young lady ought to pursue the hero. And, as many readers have
pointed out, there are no cows in the life of this cowboy—at least
none are visible in the novel. What makes the novel entertaining
and interesting is not really the formula which many students of the
western novel have attributed to Wister, but the sly fun, the
anecdotes, and the pranks which are reminiscent of Mark Twain.
In any case, *The Virginian* was a best seller in 1902, and Roosevelt
wrote to its author: "I really think you have done for the plainsmen
and mountainmen, the soldiers, frontiersmen and Indians, what
nobody else but Bret Harte or Kipling could have done"—and this
was intended as a compliment. Henry James, perhaps better able to
evaluate Wister's novel, spoke of the "subject itself, so clearly and
finely felt," the "personal and moral complexion" of the hero, the
"admirable objectivity," and concluded that the novel was a "rare
and remarkable feat." What James objected to was the happy
ending, and he begged Wister not to revive the Virginian.

In trying to determine who really lit the fire under the cowboy
novel, we note that Zane Grey's *The Spirit of the Border* was the
national best seller in 1906, and that his *Riders of the Purple Sage*
made the same dubious distinction in 1912. Obviously, people
wanted to read about the hero of the western plains, this
embodiment of southern chivalry, of strength and skill, of romance
in the isolation of the wilds. Perhaps the approaching war turned
American readers toward this peculiarly American hero who
represented Good and always found some way to conquer or stave
off Evil. At such times of national crisis it is comforting to discover

a national hero with whom the reader may share success vicariously and at the same time escape from his own real-world problems. There was another hero at this time also, one who curiously represented our allies in Great Britain. Lord Greystoke, better known as Tarzan, appeared in the African jungle the same year that Lassiter rode through Deception Pass. Edgar Rice Burroughs, the creator of Tarzan, had served a stretch in the famous Seventh Cavalry and had herded cows in the West before he turned to writing. And so in 1912 the American sub-literary scene was blessed with a pair of heroes from whom it has not yet recovered: the ape-man swinging through the trees, and the cowman galloping over the plains. For a time, at least, the jungles of Africa and the plains of Western America were equally exotic.

The flood was on, even though the next western novel to become a national best seller—Max Brand's *Singing Guns*—was not published until 1938, only two years before Clark's *Ox-Bow Incident* disturbed the formula and indicated new possibilities for the cowboy novel. The years before and after 1940 saw hundreds of conventional "western" novels, most of them fun to read (I have read over 400), some very badly written, and a few possessing qualities which might be called literary. Their very titles are revealing of the kinds of things which these novels deal with—and I take some of the better ones as examples: *Blood Brother* by Elliot Arnold, *The Apache* by James Warner Bellah, *The Dice of God* by Hoffman Birney, *Montana Road* by Harry Sinclair Drago, *Red Blizzard, Yellowstone Kelly, Return of the Tall Man,* and *The Big Pasture,* all by Clay Fisher, *The Bad Lands Beyond* by Norman Fox, *Desert Guns* by Steve Frazee, *Broken Lance* and *The Big Land* by Frank Gruber, *Bugles in the Afternoon* and *The Earthbreakers* by Ernest Haycox, *No Survivors* by Will Henry, *Law Man* by Lee Leighton, *Roads from the Fort* by Arvid Shulenberger, *Mr. Big* by Robert Walsh, *Hondo* by Louis L'Amour, *The Chieftain* by Robert Payne, *The Searchers* by Alan Le May, *Valley of the Shadow* and *Only the Valiant* by Charles Marquis Warren, *Winter of the Sioux* by Robert Steelman, *Broncho Apache* by Paul Wellman, *The Violent Land* by Wayne Overholser, and *The Hostiles* by Richard Ferber. Here are cowboys, Indians, cavalrymen, settlers, army scouts, and celebrated figures such as Lt. Col. George Custer. Each of these novels, although it has some historical or literary merit, is at least similar to several hundred other novels in that it appeals to the reader who is satisfied with stereotyped characters and well-rehearsed events. There are hero and villain, good and evil, chase and capture, sun-scorched desert and snow-blown plain, the renegade white man and the noble red savage, the Christian and the Pagan, and, of course, the gun, the horse, revenge, violence, death, and an aura of moral satisfaction floating over it all.

Is it myth, or neurosis? Warren Barker, M.D., writing in *The Psychoanalytic Quarterly,* says that the western novel's reliance on stereotype has produced an indistinct authorship, and reminds us that "anonymity of authorship is a characteristic of ancient myths." The western hero, too, is anonymous, according to this theory. "Where did you come from, baby dear?" "Out of the everywhere into here." Like the nursery rhyme, suggests Dr. Barker, the western novel is a re-enacting of the basic mysteries of life, laced liberally with the usual fantasies, regressions, oedipal complexes, fears, transferences, and ego problems. Riding his phallic horse, and with his phallic pistol pointed unerringly, the cowboy avenges his father, replaces his mother, and engages villains in threats and counterthreats of castration. The end of all this is the ride into the sunset, or the wishful return to the womb. Stated in this fashion, however, the problem is no less complex: whereas the psychiatrist may see the habitual reader of "western" novels as an immature and maladjusted ego, the literary historian or the anthropologist may regard the western novel as an extension or repetition in regional terms of ancient and basic mysteries, drives, desires, and tensions. And this is myth, neither good nor bad, neither true nor false, but simply necessary. When, on occasion, the many ingredients of the western novel are brought together in a deliberate and stylized attempt to formulate or re-state the myth, we have a novel like Jack Schaefer's *Shane,* or Oakley Hall's *Warlock,* or (one that failed) Harry Brown's *The Stars in Their Courses.* Here we see direct relationships between the western novel and the morality play or the quest narrative from Malory's *Arthur.*

What is wrong with the conventional western novel is not the myth itself but the fact that it is taken for granted and exploited with a non-literary ease, so that the western landscape becomes only an accidental stage on which the medieval players may re-enact their old truth. The serious novelist, whether he writes the historical novel, the autobiographical novel, the objective novel, or the contemporary novel, is concerned with the traditions of his region, with the physical aspects of the region, and with the ways in which the region affects those people living within it. This, I take it, is what every reputable novelist does. If, in so doing, he is able to delineate characters who can speak beyond the region, or if he can locate values which transcend the immediate area in which they originate, then his work has simply done what it ought to do. It must be a cliche by now that good literature is first regional and then universal. In the American novel, do we need to mention *The Scarlet Letter, Moby Dick, Washington Square, Huckleberry Finn,* and *The Grapes of Wrath* to prove the point? The fact that the western novelist has not always gone far enough beyond the things of his region may serve to illustrate one of his major problems: because the West is relatively new, in terms of culture and social organization, the novelist must in a sense create or locate the traditions he wishes to use, and he must do so at the very same time that he uses them. Frequently, then, the collection of facts or things, toward the making of a tradition, takes precedence over the evaluation, judgment, or use of them.

A. B. Guthrie, Jr., is the prime example of the novelist who rebuilds the Old West without, in a sense, coming to terms with it. In his well-known trilogy, *The Big Sky* covers the years 1830 to 1843, *The Way West* concentrates on the year 1845, and *These Thousand Hills* takes places from 1880 to 1887. Thus, Guthrie's three novels span most of the nineteenth century, from the mountain man to the builders of town and society. The broad panorama is vivid with details, many of which come from Garrard, Ruxton, and Parkman, plus other journals. Other details, especially those of the land itself, come from Guthrie's personal experience with the West and his sensitive perceptions of the landscape. As panorama the novels work; as individual books they do not. Guthrie, like many other western writers, has a keen eye for natural details, a sharp ear for speech sounds, and a tendency toward formlessness or looseness of construction. He is less concerned with art, or form, than he is with the facts of his material.

The Big Sky is nevertheless one of the best mountain man novels, along with Fergusson's *Wolf Song,* Blake's *Johnny Christmas,* and Manfred's *Lord Grizzly.* It nicely chronicles the westward movements of a boy who has not been able to get along in the social structure of his town on the eastern side of the Mississippi. Boone

Caudill flees to St. Louis, beset along the way by the villains of "civilization." Eventually he joins up with Dick Summers, a veteran mountain man, and is cut off from organized society. His life from that point on may be regarded more or less as the "typical" life of the mountain man, and Guthrie's descriptions of the land and of this life are memorable:

> The mountains fell away behind them, reaching high and jagged into the sky and the blue of distance settling on them. Gophers heavy with the young ones they carried piped at the horses and dived underground, their tails whisking, as the horses came close. A badger, surprised, while he chewed on a dead bird, lumbered off to one side and halted on the mound of earth he had scratched up digging a hole and watched them with a slow blaze in his eyes.
>
> The feel of the country settled into Jim, the great emptiness and age of it, the feel of westward mountains old as time and plains wide as forever and the blue sky flung across. The country didn't give a damn about a man or any animal. . . . What did it care about a man . . . ? There would be other men after him and others after them, all wondering and all wishful and after a while all dead.

In *The Big Sky*, Guthrie seems to have a tight grasp on the little things, but he cannot get them into an order or pattern which might raise them to a higher level of significance. The novel is episodic and plotless; it is an impressionistic sweep of the mountain man West, a travelogue, a source book. But the author's imagination plays only upon the details, not on the concept. *The Way West* has the same faults and is not saved by the ready-made form of the journey. Like the preceding novel it provides us with a catalogue of materials, this time concerning the trail and the wagon train, but it also simply "trails off" at the end with no real theme or sense of fate to cover the sentimentalism of the last page. The closest that Guthrie comes to saying anything is a brief statement to the effect that all men are kin through their common "hurtful, anxious, hoping look . . . the bone-deep look of man." Again, the chief value of the novel is its authentic dialogue and its precise descriptions. However, if we consider the trilogy as a unit rather than as separate volumes, we can defend these first two books as preparation for the third. *These Thousand Hills* has long been considered the least successful of the three; but it is the culmination of the earlier experiences, it suggests a theme, and it is therefore the key to the trilogy. From Boone Caudill to Lat Evans a refinement of the American character is taking place, although even Lat falls short of this kind of fulfillment. Lat, however, is the tragic person, because he is on the line between the old and the new, between two ways of life which were both necessary in their own times. Lat is caught in the change from frontier to civilization, and Guthrie allows us to see some of the potential of this cultural and historical position.

The idea of refinement was not new to Guthrie. In 1943, thirteen years before Guthrie's trilogy was completed, Wallace Stegner said much the same thing in *The Big Rock Candy Mountain.* In point of time, Stegner's narrative is later than Guthrie's and might be read as the conclusion of the idea that the American westerner carries his dead unquietly within him. We are close to our past; we are made up of the roughness of Boone Caudill, the crudeness of Lije Evans, the recklessness and dreaming-foolishness of Bo Mason. To understand ourselves we must turn to our recent past and find at least a part of our identity in the scoundrels and heroes of the nineteenth-century West. The process of recovering a usable tradition is not always an easy one, and Guthrie's lack of form may perhaps be excused with the argument that he is laying the base on which other novelists will build. We would like to think, at least, that the hardness, the discipline, the fire which shapes the vision will come later.

There has been a tendency toward very long novels in the West, and often toward trilogies or even longer groupings. It is as though the western novelist is content to take his "given" forms—the travel narrative, the quest, the sense of space—and to concentrate upon his wealth of materials rather than upon the formal organization of them. Perhaps, as has been suggested, he succumbs to the irrationalities of his land of extremes, losing sight of the rational attitudes and esthetic distance which might give him better control over his subjects. In any case, we are inclined to read a western novel for its information, its evocation of the land, its historical vision, rather than for its artistic control or its meaningful form. I should like to point out, however, that a very elementary sense of form is indeed present in the western novel, and that its simplicity need not be considered detrimental.

Walter Clark, in *The Ox-Bow Incident* and *The Track of the Cat*, has used the three-part organization of the biblical passion story. In each case the resurrection is only hinted at, but the elements of the myth are there. Art Croft in *Ox-Bow* is a kind of Everyman, average in intelligence and courage, swayed by emotions even though he can occasionally see himself objectively. With the lynch mob he partakes of two days of passion and guilt, with a certain measure of punishment, and only senses that the dawn of the third day might bring a new and better life. Three days of evil in *Track of the Cat* are climaxed by the killing of the cat, but we are led to understand that salvation is not something to be achieved only once—each man and each generation must undergo the same ordeal and arrive at a personal solution. Yet, the western landscape seems particularly well-suited to the handling of this universal theme, and so space and time—both non-logical methods of organization—become the basic elements of form. The men of Ox-Bow and Bridger's Wells fluctuate in their intentions as they move into the wind and cold of the mountains. Temporarily discouraged, and tempted to give up the search for rustlers, they are then made irritable by the same winds and are driven recklessly onward, their emotional control shattered by the elements of nature. In the shadow of the tall mountains they feel small and insignificant, so that they can regain their stature only through violence enacted upon creatures of their own kind. Granted, nature is not the only force in this drama; the mob is also stirred by the commanding personality of Tetley, whose military bluster is more effective than the pleading compassion of Davies. The question of justice achieves special importance because the question is raised slightly outside the pale of established law and regulated order. Furthermore, the novel has special distinction in light of the kind of western story which had preceded it, because no strong or courageous man steps in to halt the injustice, and no gun is raised toward Tetley when an act of determined rebellion would have stopped the lynching. The situation is complicated by the degrees of guilt found in the otherwise innocent victims: one man has a questionable past, the second is irresponsible in senility, and the third has not taken the proper business precautions in the buying of cattle. These elements of the story are all plausible, in fact they are frighteningly realistic, thereby contributing to the emotional impact of the novel. Yet, we return to the myth, because there are three men killed by an unreasonable mob in the same way that Christ was killed in the company of two thieves.

The Track of the Cat, with its extensive use of the symbol, is a more complex novel than *Ox-Bow* and a larger effort to come to terms with the concept of evil. Here again the frame of the narrative is a three-day period and our attention is focused on three men. The cat seems to represent Evil, so that on one level Clark is dealing with an ancient and universal theme. But, like Moby Dick, the black cat is also an object against which men may try themselves—a testing-board. Arthur Bridges is a mystic of sorts who thinks of the land in dream-like terms which are conducive to peace and to a limited understanding of life. He is killed by the cat. Curt is earthy, practical, and completely self-confident until his mind finally betrays him during a snowstorm and he too is killed by the cat. These two men are reminiscent of frontier types, one the dreamer who had visions of the land but could not cope with everyday necessities, the other a self-reliant destroyer of the wilderness who could not think in terms of the long view or the values which go beyond the minimum necessities. When Hal, the youngest brother, is successful in killing the cat, Clark is obviously suggesting that the ideal western man must be a combination of visionary and exploiter, of new-culture white and old-culture Indian, of thinker and doer. At the moment he is a rather innocent and ignorant young man, historically, who is yet to evolve into something more spiritual and less animalistic than he is now, and who must turn to his past for help. In a passage which also illustrates the vivid images found throughout Clark's novels, Hal sees the Indian Joe Sam's print in the snow:

> Harold stopped too, to stare down. It made him uneasy to see the print of a naked human foot in snow. It wasn't right there. The split-heart print of a deer, the dots and dashes of rabbits, the fine tail line and tiny forget-me-nots of wood mice, or even the big, broken flower of a panther or a bobcat, these were all as right in snow as black letters on paper. But this complicated, unique print, not even a little like any of them, was all wrong. There was too much time forgotten between.

The evolution of man in Western America, whether it be short term or long, is of prime concern to western novelists. Harvey

Fergusson's province is the nineteenth-century Southwest, beginning with the mountain man in *Wolf Song*, published in 1927, and
continuing through four equally superb novels: *The Blood of the
Conquerors*, 1921, *In Those Days*, 1929, *Grant of Kingdom*, 1950,
and *The Conquest of Don Pedro*, 1954. Frank Waters has sensitively
recorded the cultural evolution in the Southwest, as Indian,
Spaniard, and White American come into contact with each other.
People of the Valley, 1941, shows the isolated Spanish-speaking
people of the Sangre de Cristo mountains approaching a time of
change; *The Man Who Killed the Deer*, 1942, is about Taos Indian
justice confronting the new white man's justice; and *The Yogi of
Cockroach Court*, 1947, is a melting-pot of Mexicans, Indians,
Chinese, and whites, with the conglomerate breeding which
results. Forrester Blake's first novel, *Johnny Christmas*, 1948, is set
in the Southwest in the early nineteenth century; his second,
Wilderness Passage, 1953, moves forward to the Oregon Trail and
the advent of the Mormons in Utah; and his most recent novel, *The
Franciscan*, 1963, jumps back to the seventeenth century. Paul
Horgan, after writing three novels of contemporary New Mexico
—*Main Line West* in 1936, *Far From Cibola* in 1936, and *The
Common Heart* in 1942—went back to the years following the Civil
War in *A Distant Trumpet*, 1960. And here—although there are
more examples to follow—we run into an interesting problem in
western fiction. Horgan's *Distant Trumpet* was well-received and
made into a movie, although it is not even close to *The Common
Heart* in quality of style, seriousness of intention, or significance of
theme. The reading public wants the strangeness and the nostalgia
of the past, and at times it is very difficult to determine whether a
western novelist is returning to the past for the serious reasons I
suggested earlier or whether he is going back to meet his reading
public. I shall not mention those cases in which I suspect the latter
reason, but shall instead offer two examples of the former, even
though these men also have achieved popular success with their
"historical" novels and not with their contemporary ones.

Frederick Manfred, after publishing seven novels of the American Midlands under the name Feike Feikema, has looked farther
to the west for people and events which will help him explain the
contemporary characters of the region he calls Siouxland. He has
conceived of a five-novel series which will be called *The Buckskin
Man*. Like Cooper's *Leatherstocking Tales*, Manfred's novels are

being written in an order different from the chronological order of
the subject matter. The first to appear was *Lord Grizzly*, 1954,
based on the exploits of Hugh Glass. The second, *Riders of
Judgment*, 1957, presented the Johnson County Cattle War from
the perspective of Nate Champion. *Conquering Horse*, 1959, then
went back to an earlier all-Indian era. The fourth, *Scarlet Plume*,
will be published next month; it has a captivity theme coming out
of the Sioux uprising in Minnesota. The last to be written—now in
progress—will be a novel of darkness and fate, beginning in Sioux
City and culminating in the Black Hills. Of these novels, *Conquering Horse* must certainly rank with Waters' *The Man Who Killed
the Deer* and, reluctantly, La Farge's *Laughing Boy* as the best of
the novels about the western Indian. (In my less critical moments, I
am also inclined to put in this select group *Blood Brother*, by Elliot
Arnold, a novel which is guilty of numerous literary sins but which,
like the prodigal son, I still love.) At this point, incidentally, you
will recall that I have as yet made no attempt to name the best, or
classic, cowboy novels. Frankly, I am afraid to do so, not wanting to
get into lengthy arguments with devotees of Owen Wister, Andy
Adams, Eugene Manlove Rhodes and others of whom I am equally
suspicious for one reason or another. However, if such a list were to
be drawn up, I would probably put at or near the top three recent
novels which hardly resemble each other: Manfred's *Riders of
Judgment*, Jack Shaefer's *Monte Walsh*, and Max Evans' *The
Rounders*. Had Wister done what I think he was capable of doing,
had Adams written novels, and had Rhodes been a writer, they
would undoubtedly have to be added to the list.

Manfred's *Lord Grizzly* is his only novel to become a best seller.
Although it takes advantage of one of the supreme western
adventures, which would assure a certain amount of popularity, it
is also the book in which Manfred most deliberately attacks the
problem of form. In fact, it almost suffers from too much form.
Happily, however, this condition affords us the opportunity of
looking at some structural possibilities with western material. What
I shall propose, briefly, is that form in the western novel seems to
be based upon the rhythms of the land. Mary Austin, in *The
American Rhythm*, identifies a two-beat pattern in Indian poetry
and relates it to man's two-handedness—to up and down, to light
and dark, to back and forth movements which are elemental. If one
extends this basic beat very slightly, so that from a beginning

position we count 1 and then the up and down or back and forth become 2 and 3, we have merely re-stated Aristotle's famous insistence on beginning, middle, and end. This basic rhythm permeates *Lord Grizzly*. During a fight with Indians, mountain men as they die look inward, then outward at nature and their companions, and then inward again. Hugh Glass is established in the first third of the novel as a companyero, a member of the brotherhood; in the second part he wanders off by himself, is mauled by the grizzly, and survives miraculously as an individual; in the final third he becomes uneasy in his aloneness and rejoins the group. The point of view of the novel has three stages: one is in Hugh's mind, a second is at his eyes, and the third is at a slight distance from him. Even in style, Manfred has adhered to patterns of three:

> He slept. The wind soughed up from the south and tossed the heavy cattail cobs back and forth.
> He slept. The November sun shone gently and revived the green grass in the low sloughs.
> He slept. The wind soothed softly and rustled the ocher leaves in the rushes.

When Hugh Glass feels that he is special because of his survival, three of his former companions walk in from the plains, one at a time, having survived similar ordeals. Also, there are—if you will pardon an unavoidable allusion—three bears: Hugh himself is a grizzly among men; he is mauled by a grizzly; while traveling through the Badlands he is followed by what seems to be a phantom bear, perhaps a psychological force in Hugh's mind associated with revenge and guilt. And, to return to the question of man's evolution, we note that Hugh crawls on his belly during the first stage of survival, crawls on all fours during the second stage, and walks upright during the third. That is, he resembles the three main stages of the evolutionary development of man—reptile, four-footed animal, and two-footed upright man. The basic issues in the novel are those of the individual as related to the group and revenge as opposed to forgiveness. Because Hugh Glass is able to forego his revenge, but does so without understanding his actions, he has risen to the level of the group-human, with some insight into the necessity of the brotherhood, but he has not yet achieved a status which might be called spiritual. At this point stands mankind, Manfred seems to say, and in this way a western historical novel takes on universal significance and an almost epic quality. In spite of its avowed faults, *Lord Grizzly* is one of the outstanding novels of our time. At the very least, it stands with Hemingway's *The Old Man and the Sea* and Faulkner's *A Fable*, all three of these novels published in 1954 and having the same general celebration of the endurance of man.

The dean of western writers is Vardis Fisher, a man of extremes and of continuous production. Fisher has published about twenty-five novels, falling rather easily into three groups: the Idaho novels, the historical novels, and the Testament of Man series. For authenticity and seriousness, Fisher's historical novels rank with the best. *Children of God*, a thorough and exciting tale of the Mormons, is authoritative as well as literary. *Tale of Valor*, based closely on the Lewis and Clark expedition, proposes two of Fisher's main themes—fear and hunger. These are illustrated in the historical novels through the obvious devices associated with survival on the western frontier. In the Idaho novels it is largely the isolation and the somewhat brutal behavior of his fellow men which frighten Vridar Hunter (a slight alteration of Vardis Fisher) and warp his "natural" personality. Vridar is shaped by the cruelties of the frontier, and later in life he attempts to locate the sources of man's inhumanity. Vridar's story was first told in a tetralogy: *In Tragic Life*, 1932, *Passions Spin the Plot*, 1934, *We Are Betrayed*, 1935, and *No Villain Need Be*, 1936. He also appeared in *Dark Bridwell*, 1931, as a neighbor of the Bridwells. Reprinted in paperback as *The Wild Ones*, *Bridwell* has gone through several editions but has not yet caught the attention of many literary historians. *Bridwell* is a dark and mythic novel, splashed here and there with the beauties of nature and the exuberance of natural man. Charley Bridwell is an American Lear with his sense of satisfaction in life and his tragic amazement at its destruction by the hands of his wife and son. Here are some of the most beautiful passages in American fiction as well as some of the most violent and challenging. *Bridwell* is a supremely irrational novel, although it is under careful control. Its rhythms are those of the land—mountains, forests, rushing streams, placid but destructive solitude—and its frame is the three-fold narration by Charley, his son Jed, and his wife Lela—these very repetitions setting up another rhythm.

In spite of the frequent presence of the irrational in Fisher's novels, he is a rationalist who has spent his life locating the sources of man's irrationality and superstitiousness. When he failed to come to terms with the problem in his early tetralogy, he embarked on the amazing project which appeared in twelve volumes between 1943 and 1960 under the general title, *The Testament of Man.* Beginning with the origins of man, Fisher traced his intellectual and social progress meticulously through the thirteenth century and concluded it with a rewritten and expanded version of the Vridar Hunter tetralogy—*Orphans in Gethsemane.* The series is a work of scholarship turned into fiction. Much could be said about it, but for our purposes it is enough to note that Fisher's project was designed to explain the fears, hungers, and lack of love suffered by a boy on the early twentieth-century Idaho frontier. Thus, the history of the western world (in the broad sense) is linked as tradition to the American frontier, and it is no longer possible to say that the western novel is divorced from the realities of the world-at-large. It is true, however, that the western novel has little patience (and little contact) with the whims and fashions of metropolitan society. It is a novel of the land, of primary passions, of conquest and search. Vardis Fisher, as clearly as any writer, epitomizes four major aspects of the Western American novel:

1. Reliance on nature, on the land, for functional rhythms which become one kind of form;

2. Desire to explore the past in order to illuminate and explain the present, and to provide a workable tradition for literature;

3. Susceptibility to irrationality, because of the extreme characteristics of the land in the Great Plains—Rocky Mountains region;

4. Attempt to bring the materials of the West under rational scrutiny and control.

This last matter is proving difficult, but the Western American novel is yet young, with a bright future ahead of it. It has grown tremendously in the past several decades, and I am sorely tempted at this point to introduce thirty or forty novels which surely ought to be mentioned. Instead, let us suggest some generalizations which may lead to a profitable discussion at a later time. As the novel stands now, there are differences between the one written in the eastern or metropolitan area and the one written in the semi-arid lands of the western half of the United States. These differences will not apply to every pair of novels from the two regions, but they indicate some means of making a comparison. The eastern novel is concerned with a psychological, social, or economic ordeal, with current affairs, and with a relationship of characters in time rather than space because of the confinement of space in the East. The western novel is more often concerned with physical and anthropological matters, with characters related in space. This novel is essentially timeless, except for certain historical events, and uses or attempts to create myth through archetypal characters. The eastern novel comes from the formal traditions of the eighteenth- and nineteenth-century British social novel. The western novel is rooted in medieval romance, in Malory, in the morality plays, and in the journals and travel narratives of the nineteenth-century West. The eastern novel is based on sophistication and disillusionment; the metropolitan person rebels, or pulls in, compromising eventually with society while seeking identity within his immediate group and environment. The eastern character is shaped directly by society. In the western novel characters are relatively independent and have a good deal to say about their destinies except as they are shaped by the land. The surrender is not to society but to the conditions of the land, and the western character seeks identity within the entire natural scheme of things. The eastern novel has been heavily influenced by Freud, while the western novel tends to absorb the theories of Jung. The eastern novel is *in*tensive, probing into the centers of problems which are often small and temporary. The western novel is *ex*tensive, opening outward from character into action, racial consciousness, and the almost unlimited landscape. The eastern novel is dramatic; the western novel is epic, romantic, mythic, and lyrical. The eastern novel is a people-novel, while in the western novel Nature becomes an additional character or force. The eastern novel has a pattern of people coming to terms with hell, compromising with it, remaining lost in it, or explaining it away in Freudian analyses. The western novel features the ancient pattern of destruction, the experience of hell, and ultimate rebirth. Eastern characters have conditioned fears; western characters have primitive fears. All of which proves very little, perhaps, except that the continent on which we live is large enough to permit totally different landscapes and environments, and that the literature from the various areas will of course reflect that variety. When the professional critics, most of whom live in the East, recognize this simple fact, they may be able to strip away the long-imposed stereotyped notions and come to grips with western fiction. And when the learned professors follow suit, we may find more colleges and universities offering courses in Western American literature. In the meantime, quite apart from the critics and the Britain-oriented professors, the American West is growing and maturing and producing a literature which is worthy of our serious attention.

9

The Western Short Story

J. GOLDEN TAYLOR

J. Golden Taylor, founder of the Western Literature Association, is professor of English at Colorado State University.

This brief discussion of the Western short story is an outgrowth of an informal literary project I began early in my career on the conviction that literary scholars in all regions of America (no matter what their specialties) ought to develop a mature appreciation of the literature of their own region and an understanding of the historic cultural forces that underlie it. Though I was then aware of a few Western literary highwater marks, I still approached a comprehensive and systematic reading of Western authors quite tentatively and even defensively, realizing that in the popular mind Western literature was virtually synonymous with "Western" and "horse opera." I sensed also that, as W. H. Hutchinson has put it since, ". . . the 'Western' has been the bar sinister on any American literary escutcheon for some years past." I was dissatisfied alike with this narrow cowboy stereotype of the literary and artistic mind of my native region and with what I suspected was an unjustified condescension toward Western literature by those arbiters of taste, the literary critics.

I realized that the West has produced other forms of life than the cowboy; but for my literary purposes I needed evidence that these *others* had been significantly portrayed in literature. I soon accumulated evidence galore that the damned cowboy really had no license to ride his rough-shod, gun-slinging way over the whole Western literary landscape; and I resolved to do what I could to restrict him to his legitimate range. Though the "Western" would no doubt be skewed strongly to the bad end on a literary spectrum,

A paper presented at the Western History Association Conference, Oklahoma City, October 1964, and published in the *South Dakota Review* 2, no. 1 (Autumn 1964). Reprinted by permission of the author and the *South Dakota Review*.

there are some authentic literary uses of the cowboy. In the stories of Eugene Manlove Rhodes and a few others the "Western" has sometimes risen to the level of art. But its few achievements have not been distinguishable by the popular consumer from the customarily mediocre product; and professors and critics have seldom deigned to notice. That ardent Westerner, the late Bernard DeVoto, has amusingly exaggerated the bad literary repute of the "Western" by suggesting some ten years ago from his un-Easy Chair in *Harper's* that if a professor were to turn literary critic and give serious attention to a "Western," he would run the risk of being called up for discipline before the board of governors.

My experience with Western literature has been just the opposite of DeVoto's dire prediction; and actually before his editorial was written a number of notable Western short stories and novels had already become American classics. My early rather desultory reading grew into an enthusiasm; and, like professors in many other Western universities, I organized a course in Western American literature. These courses are meeting with marked success, bringing to the attention of many advanced students an appreciation of the best of a large and diverse body of excellent writing that is eminently worthy of the careful consideration of discriminating readers everywhere. Especially popular in my course are the nature essay, poetry, the novel, and the short story.

Although thousands of Western short stories have been published in the past century or so and hundreds of them are still worth reading, there is, strange to say, no adequate collection, either text or trade edition, that is truly representative of the scope, diversity, and excellence of the Western short story. There are numerous excellent specialized collections such as those by individual authors, collections from various journals, and the annual anthologies of the Western Writers of America. But these do not serve the need of the professor who has to furnish a comprehensive text at moderate cost in portable form.

I could not help imagining that ideal book which would contain all the stories I considered indispensable. Finally, I set aside my major research on Thoreau and Hawthorne to pursue this research in the Western short story. My plans grew in no time to a volume of six hundred pages under the demands of my ideal that it be genuinely representative of the literary excellence and thematic diversity I had found in my extended reading in the Western short story. I have benefited greatly by corresponding and on occasion talking with over one hundred Western scholars and writers; and I would welcome your suggestions both on stories to be included and the categories into which I have grouped them. I realize that no two students of Western literature would agree on any listing or classification of Western short stories: and this very fact tends to corroborate my basic thesis that there is a large body of excellent Western short stories on a diversity of themes.

Here, then, are my forty representative short stories of the American West grouped in ten categories, and with brief commentary.

I. *The Indians*

1) Grandfather Out of the Past .... Noel M. Loomis
2) All the Young Men .... Oliver La Farge
3) Lapwai Winter .... Will Henry
4) María Concepción.................................Katherine Anne Porter

The American Indians have fared no better in literature than in life: they have been thoroughly misrepresented in most western fiction; and the white man has wasted their livelihood, dispossessed them of their homeland, and uprooted their culture. But while destroying the Indians the white man has been fascinated by them from the first and has studied them intensively. As a result the historical, biographical, and anthropological studies that have been made provide the basic materials for understanding the various Indian tribes, which must precede any serious literary representation of them. The writers I have chosen in this section understand and respect the particular Indians they treat, and they tell their stories from the Indians' point of view, from inside their world of values.

Noel M. Loomis personally recommended his "Grandfather Out of the Past" to me, out of the hundreds of stories he has written, when I told him I was looking for Western short stories that dealt with Indians responsibly. He is Texas born and a descendant of pioneers; and he knows the West Texas Comanche country where the story is set. He is a master of authentic Comanche lore, with which the story is richly furnished; and his story becomes a classic rebuke of those who represent Indians of any tribe in cliché terms. Tuchubarua, the main character, old in body but strong in his reverence for traditional Comanche morality, defends himself and his granddaughter from a malignant enemy by heroically mustering in a dramatic climax the moral courage to denounce this enemy who has broken a Comanche sex taboo. In this story Loomis has achieved a warmly sympathetic and psychologically penetrating study in integrity.

The late Oliver La Farge, of *Laughing Boy* fame, is likely the supreme interpreter of the Navajo Indians. "All the Young Men," like several of his other stories, deals with the deterioration of the Navajo under the impact of the white man. This story begins near the end of Old Singer's life, when he is in the last stages of decline; contrasting with this state are the scenes of his youth provided in stream-of-consciousness flashbacks. Landing finally in jail, his medicine bundle with its sacred jewels desecrated by his jailors, he desperately and ever more poignantly seeks escape from reality in fervently conjured-up images as he sings his prayers and thinks of the days when with all the young men he rode the Navajo trail of beauty.

"Lapwai Winter" has its setting in the valleys and mountains of the Snake and Clearwater rivers of Idaho and eastern Oregon, the ancestral home of the Nez Perce Indians. The action takes place in the late 1870's when Chief Joseph desperately tried to preserve his people after a bald repudiation of their treaty left them destitute. The story is narrated with dignity and restraint in the first person by Heyets (Mountain Sheep), a Nez Perce boy of fourteen who, at the insistence of the Indian Agent, is to be educated at the agency school near Fort Lapwai. Heyets is unimpressed with the Christianized civilization he has observed, and he fights with what means he has to prevent the destruction of the tribal culture in the tribe's future leaders. Chief Joseph looms out in the story in his historic grandeur (one of the noblest of all Indian chieftains) as "that strange, sad-eyed man who almost never smiled." The best way to read "Lapwai Winter" is with a print of the J. C. Curtis photograph of Chief Joseph at hand; then a memorable story becomes hauntingly unforgettable, for the dignity and despair that pervade the story are seen in every line of his face.

"María Concepción" is one of Katherine Anne Porter's earliest short stories and one of her best. According to her essays about her experiences in Mexico, she both understood and respected the Mexican Indians among whom she lived on her extended visits. In this semi-Christianized culture, María Concepción lives somewhat apart from the community in her remote *jacal* with her philandering young husband, who works occasionally for an American archaeologist. But she is also apart from the group in spirit, for she cares tremendously, as the mass of people do not, about the quality of the life she leads. Proud of her Christianity, she nonetheless does what her primitive nature demands to protect what is of most value to her—and, as it turns out, to the women of her society and, perhaps, to the human race. Her struggles and agonies are presented from the inside; the women of the town, who finally see her as their champion, are pictured only from without. In the last scene nature is shown to be in harmony with the powers that sustain the human institutions which in turn preserve the species.

II. *The Mountain Men and the Troopers*

5) When a Document Is Official .... Frederic Remington
6) Mountain Medicine .... A. B. Guthrie, Jr.
7) The Unbeliever .... Dorothy M. Johnson
8) Bound for Taos .... Harvey Fergusson

The mountain men, some one hundred years after their demise, likely carry the most romantic connotations of any figures in the annals of the West. DeVoto writes about them with a nostalgic ardor; and Dale Morgan says, "They seem now like a race of giants in a golden age, though no one of them was exempt from having to earn a living." Note how he characterizes a few of the most renowned of these giants: "Among them is the intelligent, mule-tough, religiously inclined Jedediah Smith. The lank, Jackson-faced, durable, consistently fortunate William L. Sublette. The ruddy-featured Thomas Fitzpatrick, with his iron control over a volcanic nature. The quiet, ever-dependable David E. Jackson. The stripling Jim Bridger, destined to become the supreme master of the wilderness. The swarthy-featured, irascible, self-sufficient, yarn-spinning Moses 'Black' Harris, and countless others whose names evoke spectacular events or exploits—Hugh Glass, he of the misadventure with the grizzly."

The troopers, along with regular infantry and mounted infantry, had the inglorious duty of carrying out the systematic extermination of the plains, mountain, and desert Indians who stood in the way of progress. In these four stories, therefore, the authors focus primarily upon the mountain men and army men as heroes; and the Indians are seen essentially in the conventional role as the chief enemies the mountain men had to circumvent in their search for beaver and as obstructions to the westward-encroaching settlers.

I suppose no one would question the idea that Frederic Remington has left the best drawings and paintings there are of troopers and their mounts, Indians, and mountain men; and like C. W. Russell, he was not content with one art but made fictional portraits of the same characters. He was a close friend of Wister and illustrated his books and wrote exuberant letters to him. His "When a Document Is Official" shows an unusually high quality of dedication in a trooper on the frontier service during the campaign against Sitting Bull and Crazy Horse. This trooper, newly promoted, after nine "freezing, grilling, famishing years," to officer's rank, carries an important message for his colonel, has a run-in with buffalo hunters, and as the Sioux close in on him faces an interestingly ironic dilemma.

A. B. Guthrie, Jr., thoroughly and happily of Montana, who has treated the mountain man with some thoroughness in *The Big Sky,* has dealt with him also in his shorter fiction. His "Mountain Medicine" has its setting in the Three Forks area, where John Colter and John Potts, having been released from the Lewis and Clark Expedition on its return journey, settled down as mountain men to hunt beaver. It follows the historical account rather closely, changing Potts' and Colter's names to Potter and Clell respectively, inventing the beaver-lodge hide-out, and of course building a dramatically effective story out of the raw materials of history and legend. Defending himself in his foreword against accusations of plagiarism, Guthrie wrote: "I made fiction of Bradbury's account, staying as close to the record as the short-story form seemed to permit. If they accuse me now, I won't answer. History is there for the writer of fiction, else we have to burn a lot of books."

Dorothy Johnson, also a Montanan, peoples her stories about the region where she grew up with mountain men, Indians, and troopers who are vividly individualized; and she plots actions that are filled with suspense masterfully controlled. In "The Unbeliever" she has created an unusually complex frontier derelict, Mahlon Mitchell, named Iron Head by the Crows, a sort of combination of Parkham's amusing Tete Rouge and Hamlet. Somewhere deep in Mitchell's opportunist body is a relentlessly accusing conscience, ego, or soul that compels him to attempt at least a modest self-redemption. This he aims to do by acting as

scout and interpreter for an army troop going to make peace with
the Crows, the very tribe with whom he had lived and raised a
family—and deserted. In a wondrously ironic climax Iron Head
discovers too late that he was all along of great value to the
Indians, but he is unable to profit by his new-found status.

Harvey Fergusson, like Guthrie, has dealt with the mountain
man in novels but concerns himself with those of the Southwest.
"Bound for Taos" is slight in plot but interesting in its revelation of
the long periods of hardship in the mountains followed by the
annual outbursts when the mountain men bring their furs to
market. Their lusty natures are revealed chiefly through dialogue
that is at once realistic and poetic:

"How Mexican women loved hard-riding, Indian-killing gringos,
full of lust and money!

Ho, you *muchachas*, get ready for big doins!

Wash off the red stain of *alegria* that saves your faces from the
sun.

Put on your bright red skirts and white *camisas*.

Hang silver and gold on your necks and arms.

Limber your legs for dancing and wear roses in your hair.

Here come mountain men hell-bent for a spree."

III. *The Treasure Seekers and the Tricksters*

The treasure seekers of the West have written one of the most
frenzied chapters in all its flamboyant past. Thoreau was disdainful
of them as well-employed men who abandoned life in trying to get
something for nothing. Poe found in El Dorado one of his most apt
symbols for mortal man's frustration in this world. Twain, somewhat ambivalent, nevertheless participated in the frenzy, became a
millionaire for a week, and left in *Roughing It* an on-the-spot
account of its fever and failure.

"All-Gold Canyon," though one of Jack London's most popular
stories, is still one of his best in its careful structuring, suspense, and
tone. In the Sierra setting of this story, idyllic nature is intruded

upon by a pocket miner who, while defacing the mountain side in locating a rich pocket, is silently observed by the patient trickster who sees in the hard-working miner an easy mark. London shows successively the cycle of man's rapacious presence in nature: idyll, intrusion, treasure, violence, the idyll again. It is an interesting anticipation of Clark's "Indian Well."

J. Frank Dobie, profound and revered dean of the interpreters of the Southwest, has written one of the most fascinating short tales of lost treasure—in a region filled with lost mines. It is a sort of Western gothic in its suggestions of the supernatural with voices and dreams.

Ray B. West recommended "The One and Only Appearance of Jeez Christ on Sun Mountain" to me. He had first published Jarvis Thurston's story in the *Rocky Mountain Review* in 1945. It is a notable achievement in vernacular narrative, told in the first person ostensibly by an old timer of the Virginia City (Nevada) heyday. Sun Mountain is an earlier name for Mt. Davidson, which rises above Virginia City. The story achieves a dimension of universality comparable to Clark's "The Wind and Snow of Winter" in portraying a treasure seeker, gradually destroyed by the harsh and lonely life, floating mentally and emotionally out of the world of reality into one of more comfortable illusion and realization. The stories differ in the turn Thurston gives to his quondam treasure seeker: he has the illusion that he is Jesus Christ—who is supposed to have said something about treasures to be found in heaven rather than those that are found in the earth. The profane and barbaric practical jokers of Virginia City can imagine nothing more funny than to hear this deranged old man lecture. This story is a tremendous experience.

Mark Twain's "The Celebrated Jumping Frog of Calaveras County" precipitated him into a public attention he did not entirely appreciate. He wrote to his mother the following year: "To think that, after writing many an article a man might be excused for thinking tolerably good, those New York people should single out a villainous backwoods sketch to compliment me on!" He had heard the rudiments of the story in the gold fields of California; "the thing happened in Calaveras County in the spring of 1849." Forty-five years later he met Professor Van Dyke of Princeton who explained to him that the original of the story was a Greek legend two thousand years old. Indeed the idea of the

trickster is not new, but Mark Twain makes his version yield a new
dimension by his skilled incorporation of four humorous techniques:

(1) the use of vernacular, which is humorous because of the
disparity between standard English and varied distortions; (2) the
use of the trickster, playing a joke, getting a friend into some kind
of boring, painful, or embarrassing situation, preferably a situation
that undermines dignity or deflates pride; (3) the use of senile
garrulity, the aimless, incoherent reminiscences of an old man with
a hop-scotch mind; and finally, the use of paradox, the idea that
pride is not really a strength but a weakness: "Pride goeth before
destruction and a haughty spirit before a fall." (Pro. 16:18) Twain
(who liked to make more devastating commentaries about "the
damned lousy human race") is here content to smile at his country
bumpkin's prideful self-assurance about frogs and show how this
pride makes him an easy mark for a trickster of moderate sense.

IV. *The Entrepreneurs and the Gamblers*

Entrepreneurs and gamblers are not unrelated to treasure
seekers and tricksters. The restaurant owner with whom I eked out
a subsistence while in college during the depression years used to
quip proudly to me: "There are tricks in every trade but the
restaurant business—but it's just one big trick!" In one sense every
business is a gamble (including Western farming, ranching—and
even banking, till the federal government became ensurer of prices
and deposits); the gambler is to some extent a trickster, yet he is
also an individual enterpriser; and the treasure seeker is self-
reliance itself, gambling his life and his luck against nature.

In "Baker's Bluejay Yarn" Twain has created a remarkable fable,
for his focus is man's foibles, not the energetic bird that tries to fill a
cabin with acorns. It is actually a satire on the foolishness of
mankind—particularly in the acquisitive instinct, man's urge for
more security than he can possibly use. Twain, with his bird, plays
up the entrepreneur's skill in self-deception and rationalization.
This same man, turned congressman, palliates his conscience for
wholesale graft while convincing himself that he is really serving

the public interest. The jay finally enacts in the fable Twain's amusement with man's lack of ordinary sense (much less empirical or rational investigation) in resorting to temper and profanity.

"The Right Eye of the Commander" is one of Harte's lesser-known stories of California life. It focuses upon an interesting contrast of two cultures that actually met historically—the fabled Spanish missions along *El Camino Real* and the masters of far-ranging Yankee merchant ships, essentially glorified New England peddlers, who came to trade and did well. H. G. Rogers, Jedediah Smith's companion, recorded a situation very like the setting of this story when he and Smith visited San Gabriel Mission in 1826. He saw a prosperous establishment, thousands of converted Indians doing the labor and studying Christianity, and a Yankee trading ship in the harbor. Harte does little with the Catholic enslavement of the Indians that attracted Rogers' notice, but he builds his story around the Indians' superstition. They are unable to account for the miracle of the Senor Commandante's suddenly appearing with a new glass eye in his long-blind socket—just one of the many indications of the Yankee trader's salesmanship.

Harte's other story, "The Outcasts of Poker Flat," has his characteristic weaknesses, but still does some things well. Harte here indulges in an almost perverse reversal of character stereotypes: whereas gamblers and prostitutes are popularly depicted as all bad, he is not content till he has made them saints and saviors. The stalwarts of the town who advocated hanging the outcasts have less concern for the law than the profit. With all his lack of realism he tells an effective, though sentimental, story, with good ironic and humorous touches, such as when he has "the deported wickedness" join the innocents in singing a fervent camp-meeting hymn: "I'm proud to live in the service of the Lord,/ and I'm bound to die in His army."

Stephen Crane is noted for his pessimistic philosophy about man and nature, and he writes with a realistic emphasis far from Harte's romantic approach. In "The Blue Hotel," with a frontier Nebraska setting, Crane brings coincidentally together a group of people—including gamblers and entrepreneurs—and shows how each unwittingly acts in such a way as to become involved in a murder. There is a relentless cause and effect in operation for Crane in man and in nature. The irony that fear produces provocative arrogance in the Swede, which in turn brings enmity from total strangers, is merely

Crane's way of interrelating coincidental and causal forces. The full irony is not apparent till part IX of the story, laid months later, when the Easterner tries to explain to the cowboy how "We are all in it!"

V. *The Outlaws and the Lawmen*

The Old West provided unusual scope for the talents of innumerable outlaws; and, though the glamour seems to have centered more on the outlaws than the lawmen (witness Billy the Kid and Pat Garrett), almost every outlaw sooner or later met his well-deserved end. Biographies and historical studies of these characters and their conflicts are almost without number, but the fictional elaborations stagger the imagination!

Crane's "The Bride Comes to Yellow Sky" seems to have achieved virtually the status of a classic in this area. Almost every person with whom I have corresponded or talked about Western stories in the past two years has recommended this story. It is starkly simple in its development and has none of the undertow of naturalistic philosophy which characterizes most of Crane's other writing.

Jack London's "To the Man on Trail," unlike his "All-Gold Canyon," emphasizes a naturalistic philosophy—that man is basically an animal whose nature is determined entirely by his heredity and environment. Under conditions such as those in the Klondike, man's veneer of civilized social responses is sloughed off, and his animal will to survive, to achieve his ends outside the law and traditions of ordered society, takes over. Man and nature are anarchistic in London's view. The Malemute Kid and his companions, following this operation of nature, help Westondale escape and shout, "Confusion to the Mounted Police!" Westondale embodies the same philosophy.

Max Brand's "Wine on the Desert" is a jewel in construction, theme, and execution. Durante, like Hemingway's killers—or, in a larger sphere, like Melville's Claggart—is incarnate evil. It would take half a day merely to identify the involuted ironies that are worked into the revenge that Tony and nature take upon Durante.

Those who are enthusiastic about Eugene Manlove Rhodes and those who are not form one of the deepest dichotomies among students of Western literature. In "Pasó por Aquí" Rhodes has compressed much of his love of the New Mexico country where he lived as almost exactly the kind of humane horseman that he portrays in this story; much of the action happened in one form or another to him or his friends. The title, which means "passed by here," was used by many who ventured into the unknown reaches of the West, usually appending their names and dates. The title readily lends to the story a parabolic dimension of man's journey through life and what it amounts to; and the parts of the story that are narrated by Monte in a kind of Spanish English support this emphasis by repeatedly echoing the pertinent parables of Jesus. Here, as elsewhere in his fiction, Rhodes is celebrating his most cherished conviction that the pioneering friends he knew in New Mexico were some of the most inherently noble men in the world. The fleeing robber who forgets himself and helps nurse back to life a Mexican family stricken with diphtheria on a remote ranch he chances upon in his flight is Rhodes' central character and the means of embodying his theme. Pat Garrett, much maligned killer of Billy the Kid, appears in the story as a morally imaginative sheriff who finds important areas of justice outside of and above the letter of the law.

VI. *The Cowboys and the Horsemen*

The cowboy seems to have originated in Texas and to have flourished in his pure state from Texas to Montana for not more than about thirty-five years following the Civil War—and his interpreters of every variety have flourished ever since. I do not claim to be one of these experts, though at eight I was one of the most accomplished horsemen and herders of cows for my size in the whole region roundabout southern Alberta and northern Montana. Perhaps I had better say little more, for I have let my skill lapse—and in Oklahoma I am, after all, pretty close to Texas where the experts grow. The four stories that I have selected from among the works of writers who are surely the most authentic portrayers of the cowboy in fiction emphasize what the experts insist were some of his most characteristic qualities: (1) his generosity to comrades, (2) his humor, (3) his love of life on the open range and remorse and nostalgia at its passing, and (4) his love of good horses and the challenge of breaking and training them. Adams' "In the Hands of His Friends" develops this camaraderie and generosity among cowboys by showing a group from a Texas ranch help their crippled cook, little Jack Martin, establish himself as a home-steader. The setting which quite excitingly makes this possible is the opening of the Oklahoma Strip at high noon, April 22, 1889. Adams captures the fever of the occasion, shows the cowboys dealing forthrightly with a Sooner, and portrays exuberantly the housewarming for their friend, with its food, drinks, dancing, and courting.

In "A Corner in Horses" White uses an Arizona range campfire for a frame setting wherein Sacatone Bill tells a humorous vernacular tale to some forty cowboys gathered around. It is a virtuoso performance and involves the elaborately contrived ven-geance of Dutchy, a saloon keeper in Cyanide, Colorado, upon his tormentor, the Irishman O'Toole.

Though there is typically a strain of humor in most of Wister's cowboy stories, in "At the Sign of the Last Chance" what humor there is is subdued. The story is his major treatment of the demise of the open range and the old life of the cowboy. It is a dirge, in which several old timers who meet at an inn commiserate with each other and an Eastern visitor of other times.

"Corazón" is reputed to be the best story ever written about a horseman and a horse.

VII. *The Ranchers and the Homesteaders*

The flood of land-hungry homesteaders upon the public domain (much of it very recently the homeland of Indians) was treated by Andy Adams; but he showed none of the bitterness of the conflict between the homesteader, who thought he had good title to public land, and the rancher, who considered the open range his own.

Conrad Richter and Luke Short have written essentially parallel stories of this struggle, both set in the Southwest.

"Lutie," told in the first person by a narrator emotionally involved, achieves intensity and poetic dimension, as indicated in the opening sentence: "That lusty pioneer blood is tamed now, broken and gelded like a wild horse and a frontier settlement." The nostalgia for the romantic grandeur of the past picks up when the narrator says of his uncle, once owner of a proud cattle kingdom: "His rude empire is dead and quartered today like a steer on the meat block, but I still lie in bed at night and see it tossing, pitching, leaping in the golden sunlight of more than fifty years ago, sweeping up to his very door, stretching a hundred and twenty miles north and south along the river, and rolling as far into the sunset as stock could roam—a ranch larger than Massachusetts with Connecticut thrown in, his fabulous herds of Texas cattle, sprinkled like grains of cinnamon across the horizons, his name a legend. . . ." In sharp realistic contrast to this grandeur are the violent means used to stop the influx of homesteaders, the anxious and tired and discouraged people in the covered wagon trains of land seekers, and the court scene, a travesty of justice. "Court Day" is involved in this same basic struggle. It presents more direct action and less poetic intensity: it reveals a similar corrupt sheriff and court, pliable to the powerful; it emphasizes the outlaw nature of cattlemen who defied the law of the land.

"Ike and Us Moons" is set on a horse ranch in northeastern Wyoming and, as the title indicates, is narrated in the vernacular. Remnants of a post–Civil War Kentucky feuding family and an orphan, Ike, find their ultimate values in family loyalty and the preservation of the family heritage in the land. Ike's simple and primitive solution reaches a climax of such proportions that it has led one noted critic to suggest that "probably this is one of the finest stories written in America."

"The Homestead Orchard" is just one of many fine stories which H. L. Davis has set in Oregon's mountain valleys. It involves a young man's struggle to achieve maturity in a society where he has a reputation for instability. He is found herding his father's sheep in a drought year and is forced to take them for pasturage to the very homestead his father had lost on his account. A tense scene threatening the use of a folk-method employed by cattlemen in disposing of troublesome sheepmen—dragging them behind a horse, tied up on a large jute woolsack—provides the climax. When his son comes through and he discovers that the orchard has not died, the old man observes: "I know how it feels to have something you've raised turn out better than you expected."

VIII. *The Farmers and the Townspeople*

The farmers and townspeople, who form such important segments of Western life, have been the subject of much good fiction. With the struggles of the nesters forgotten, the open range plowed, fenced, and irrigated, the crude frontier settlements transformed into comfortable, orderly towns, life in the rural West grew naturally into a newer set of problems such as those dealt with sensitively in the present stories: assimilation of the immigrant, cultural stagnation in an isolated folk group, small-town Christian conservatism, and the development of self-reliance in the younger generation.

"Neighbor Rosicky," the warmly affectionate tribute of Willa Cather to the gentle Czech immigrants she had known from childhood in the vicinity of Red Cloud, Nebraska, has for thirty years been one of America's best loved stories. Rosicky is the most charming immigrant in American literature, and his genius lies in a rare quality of parental love that knows no selfish ends.

It has been my pleasure through a long friendship with Juanita Brooks to encourage her to write "The Outsider" and other stories based on the life she knew in the Mormon village of Bunkerville, Nevada. It was first published in *Journal of American Folklore* for July–September, 1964; the editor, John Greenway, has provided an elaborate introduction. Nothing can be more simple than the experience she recounts of the coming of a cultivated outsider to her isolated community where every human value was to be found "in the Great Plan of establishing the Kingdom of God upon earth and making the desert blossom." Likewise, the implications are universal for all the parochial who get a glimpse of the riches of human culture to be found in books, colleges, and travel.

Mr. John's title, "Neither Jew Nor Greek," is obviously an echo of that distressingly all-inclusive brotherly love that is the culmination of the Judeo-Christian ideal of the worth of all men. It is a problem still, I presume, in large as well as small towns, and perhaps in places other than Colorado, the setting of this version.

Wallace Stegner's "Chip Off the Old Block" is apparently drawn upon the small-town life he knew when he lived in Saskatchewan just across the line from Montana at the time of the flu epidemic during World War I. The chip off the old block is Chet, a fourteen-year-old youngster, whose family has been hospitalized with the flu. He has been told "to hold the fort," whose most interesting ammunition is a wagonload of whiskey of assorted varieties, which his father had just brought in from Montana. Chet survives the silent vigil in the empty house, outwits some scoundrels who try to steal the whiskey, and then unstintingly dispenses it in an impromptu party for an hilarious assortment of the townspeople—his *father's* friends. The return and reconciliation of father and son provide the climax; and Stegner probes around with some awareness and intelligence in that chasm which always separates two generations of a family.

IX. *The Hunters and Hunted*

Walter Van Tilburg Clark's story, "Hook," is in a class by itself. On one level it is a sort of natural history of that arch-predator, the hawk; but Clark has individualized and personalized Hook so that his story is heightened into a saga of one child of nature, who is at once brave and beautiful and terrible. The nearest thing to it are some poems by Jeffers, like "Hurt Hawks," that similarly celebrate the killing instinct as the hawk's life blood and evoke the sheer beauty of the hawk soaring over the California setting from coast range and valley to Pacific. I suspect most readers of the story feel a mild shock when they realize the degree of their identification with Hook.

Paul Horgan's "To the Mountains" is a gripping tale on the level of sheer adventure in hunting, but the author obviously set out to make it much more. He has made it a stirring re-enactment of the ritual, old as man, by which the child assumes responsibility and faces whatever danger presents itself in order to become a man.

With their father away in Mexico trading in the autumn of 1800, two brothers, Louis, sixteen, and Julio, thirteen, leave their poor home in the hills near Bernalillo (in what is now New Mexico) and go to the mountains to get furs to supply the family's dire need. Surviving a two-day snow and ten days of peril and exhaustion, they return, men; and everyone realizes that something new—yet very old—has happened.

Zane Grey's reputation—such as it is—is in novels and on subjects other than hunting; but his "Don: The Story of a Lion Dog" is an excellent saga of a dog who loved freedom and hated men. The narrator sets out to celebrate "the greatness of a dog," as he puts it. He tells how he finally won the love of the dog in saving its life—and how it ultimately saved his. The setting is the rugged and colorful Colorado River country around the Grand Canyon.

"The Last of the Grizzly Bears" is not in itself a hunting story, but Ray B. West apparently draws upon his boyhood experiences with grizzlies in Yellowstone Park and his memories of seeing the remains of Old Ephraim, the gigantic grizzly that Frank Clark killed in Logan Canyon in 1923. In the story these boyhood confrontations and memories become the ironic contrasting mirror in which the disillusioned organization man sees the truth about the predatory society in which he functions as a corporation lawyer in an Eastern city.

X. *The Contemporary Westerner*

The contemporary westerner is pretty much a part of the human race. He is about as widely traveled and as well educated as the average American, and he has contrived to build about the same sort of physical and spiritual world. "The West That Was" (as Rhodes described in 1922 the old West he had known) gave way some time ago to the West that is: standard American civilization complete with slums, subdivisions, service clubs, ancestor-worshiping societies, and advertising. There are some indications that if we are to survive at all we had better keep our sense of humor in repair.

"Laughter," by Vardis Fisher, centers around a minister preaching a funeral sermon. When, after some time, he sees in the audience the man he has been lamenting so eloquently, he stops short and bursts out, "Who the hell is dead around here?!" Anybody from Utah would know that this is an adaptation from an actual incident in the life of J. Golden Kimball, who has been called by John Greenway "the most famous—or infamous—Mormon divine . . . that most outrageous preacher in the history of Christendom." J. Golden Kimball is perhaps the most refreshing character in the folklore of the West.

William Saroyan has exploited the humor and pathos of his Armenian family and friends in California in innumerable stories. "The Pomegranate Trees" deals with his Uncle Melik, the imaginative and poetic and esthetic agriculturist who purchased a piece of worthless desert land at the foot of the Sierra Nevada Mountains, planted hundreds of young pomegranate trees, and then counted his pomegranates much too soon.

"The Apostate," by George Milburn, deals with a man who has quit his Rotary Club—not his church. The story is in the form of a monologue in which the speaker is explaining to a fellow Rotarian why he has withdrawn his membership: his son's fraternity brothers at the university do not approve. The monologist is unaware of the irony that he has described identical values and rituals in the two brotherhoods.

Steinbeck's "The Leader of the People" is a fitting counterpart to "Grandfather Out of the Past," with which I began my paper: both show the integrity of older members of society as well as those of a later generation who do not respect them. Steinbeck's story engages the reader in witnessing a most painful breach of piety—lack of respect for an old man who lived courageously, leading the people through danger and the unknown to the land that Tiflin, as a rancher, now takes for granted. Jody's grandfather emerges in a dignity which is in striking contrast to Tiflin's crassness and impiety.

o   o   o

My assumption all along has been that one might reasonably expect that the literature of a region would have some resemblance to the lives of its people—that all life is the legitimate province of the literary artist. In my paper I have been chiefly concerned to give evidence that many facets of Western life have been admirably represented in the short story.

I should like to see America's Western writers in the decades ahead draw even more resourcefully than they have in the past upon the whole gamut of Western life which is, after all, a significant part of the American experiment. Perhaps we need to remind ourselves of the observation of James Bryce in 1891 that ". . . the West is the most American part of America; that is to say, the part where those features which distinguish America from Europe come out in strongest relief." (II, 697)

America has a good deal of unfinished business on its hands, social and literary; and it may be that the West has some unique contribution to make to the whole society. There is something of this, and a good deal more, in Wallace Stegner's article in the January 1964 *Atlantic*, "Born a Square—The Westerner's Dilemma," which, in closing, I heartily recommend to you.

10

The "Western Story" as Literature

W. H. HUTCHINSON

W. H. Hutchinson, professor of history at California State University, Chico, is the biographer and bibliographer of Eugene Manlove Rhodes, as well as the literary executor of the Rhodes estate.

I

The truly opinionated reader is likely to be a happy man. Whenever the world in its dank majesty is too much with him, he has sure surcease. Bringing his self-honing prejudice to a keen edge, he can retire to his literary woodshed to split an infinitive or six in his sacred cause and invariably return indoors with a basketful of seasoned chips that burn before his chosen shrine with a clean, blue flame.

When he obeys some lemming-like instinct towards generous sharing and carts these self-same chips to his neighbor's hearth, the fact that they fill the room with smoke or spit corrosive sparks on the installment broadloom bothers him not at all. They burn all right at home and the neighbor's chimney probably needs cleaning and he ought to sink his hearth below floor level. However, let these chips from my basket burn on your hearth and may they give pleasant if pyrotechnic warmth.

When it comes down to the literature produced under the bar sinister, "western story," even the most opinionated reader will do well to burn his chips only at home, preferably when the rest of the family have gone out for an intellectual refresher at the nearest Hollywood outlet.

In the first place, you have to define what you mean by the American West. Then you must document what you mean by the literature of your definition. If you become a practitioner of the Black Arts in the process, it is quite understandable and the author invites the exchange of trade secrets with special emphasis on waxen images of the less opinionated.

Specifically, the West I know, the West-That-Was, is an entity in time and space quite easily defined. For a period of thirty-five years at most, from Appomattox to the turn of the century, it stretched from the One Hundredth Meridian to the Sierra-Cascade summit between the Rio Grande border line and the equally unfortified line of Milk River. In fine, it was the Cattle Kingdom defined by Walter Prescott Webb. Its miners, politicos, and merchants were adjuncts to a society based on livestock.

The whole Pacific littoral west of the dividing ranges is excluded from this entity and for good reason. The Pacific slope was linked to the Eastern seaboard, to the entire civilized world, by ship, Pony Express, Overland Stage, Telegraph, and Silver Palace Cars while the West was still *terra incognita*. The Pacific slope acted and reacted upon the world and the seat of government while the West was still a captive province. Finally—Chambers of Commerce please note—the Pacific slope enjoyed a marked climatic difference and it had trees, whole forests of green, living giants that were an integral part of its economy just as trees had been an integral part of the economy in the lands whence the people of the Pacific slope had come. To sum up—the West was what you passed through to reach California or the Oregon Country. It still is!

Having achieved our definition of the land, we have no reasonable excuse for begging the question of literature it produced. The easiest way to define this literature would be to expropriate Bingham Canyon and into it cast one copy of everything ever written on the subject. This would cover the field, from Congressional documents through foreign observations down to the latest copy of "Gunsmoke Yarns" on the corner newsstand. No one would be slighted and the seeker after a true definition of Western Literature could be tolled over to the brink with a carroty jargon and shoved. However, since industry still needs the products of the Pit and homicide laws are rigidly interpreted, we are reduced to mere words.

In a valiant effort to reduce the area of possible confusion, let it stand here that the subject of western literature may be divided, with Gaul, into three parts:

(a) Interpretation, as in a recognized field of research such as history, economics, politics, sociology, religion, etc.
(b) Documentation, as in the reporting of daily life and events, folkways, arti-crafts, etc.
(c) Fiction, as in the literarily suspect "western story."

And, even as Caesar, let us pass quickly over the first two parts to reach the meat in our coconut.

Under the first heading are found the facts, figures, and causative forces that provide the skeletal reconstruction of this distinct era in American life. I think that one man and one book may stand for the whole body of material. The man is Walter Prescott Webb and the book is his *The Great Plains*. Not only is this a monumental and capable effort to assess the whole entity we have defined but it is the work of a scholar with a feeling heart and it possesses a cross-fertilizing influence of great value. It is the best example of what I comprehend my first grouping to have contributed to western literature. If it serves its exemplary purpose, no other citation is needed. If it does not, no amount of citations can do other than confuse the issue.

In the second group, you strike a slightly richer vein of disputation as to meaning. However, there should be little argument over what is meant by this group if you take as examples Charley Russell with *Trails Plowed Under,* or Teddy Blue with *We Pointed Them North,* or such as Will James, Ross Santee, Mary Kidder Rak, and—with blare of trumpet—J. Frank Dobie. I would add, also, the song collections of John and Alan Lomax and the poetry of Badger Clark and Jack Thorp. These men and the things they set down before it was too late reflect the life, artifacts, and customs of the people of our time—space entity from the human level of everyday life. In some of them, particularly in Dobie, the work has a seasoning of folklore and a breath of man's soul that transcends description. It should be in a grouping of its own—and it is in my heart.

It is the third group, the "western story" fiction, that contains what I believe to be the only literature of the West-That-Was deserving of the capital. It is in this group, the fiction, that you find the only writing of the cattle kingdom which Bernard DeVoto says "reaches a level which it is intelligent to call art." It is only in this fiction that the artists have fixed forever the time, place, and people who never were before and will never be again.

II

The fiction of the West was written, and still is, for the same reason that most fiction starts out in life—to provide entertainment for the reader and economic security for the writer. The bulk of western ficion was written, and still is, by those who wrote from the *outside in;* that is, they wrote of a region, time, and people with whom they had nothing in common save as material passing under their microscope. Also, the bulk of western fiction was written, and still is, for a majority audience who knew and know nothing of the region, time, and people being served up to them.

These two factors are no great matter from the standpoint of reader appeal, writer's scope, or publisher's sales. If most readers knew nothing of the West-That-Was, it follows that they lacked criteria by which to judge the true quality of what they read. If it pleased them, if it lifted them out of themselves for a brief moment, then the writer had served his primary purpose of entertainment and, perhaps, his own purse. Since the writer was writing from the *outside in* for people who lived on the *outside*, the writings were but two-dimensional, lacking depth, because the readers could understand this art form and demanded it. This brings us to the factor that most influenced western fiction.

The writers knew the people who composed their market (audience) far better than they knew the people of whom they wrote. It is the same today. Any writer worth the title, who hopes to make a livelihood with pen or portable, knows just as much about his audience as he does about his material, if not far more. He has to because if he does not, it is—commercially—a waste of his time, his agent's time and the time of many editors; this leads to an inconvenient shortness of tempers all around. It follows that the bulk of western fiction, from novelist through slick writer to pulpeteer, has aimed at a definite audience and grooved his material to fit.

For example, take the early stories (he called them "sketches") of Bret Harte. These were not a part of the time-space culture which here concerns us: neither were Mark Twain's stories of slightly later date: but they did set the pattern which still survives with inevitable mutations. They were caricatures of reality as indeed they had to be, because the people for whom they were intended could not or would not try to understand the reality itself.

Harte and Twain applied unquestioned skill to a certain scene through which they passed and depicted it so that their audience could grasp it easily. They could have done the same with any time, scene, or people; and Twain, in particular, did. They contributed to American Literature but not to the Literature of the West. I recently studied a Hollywood story treatment which combined four of Harte's sketches to make one single story line for filming. It was a film that depended upon action, scene, and Technicolor for its eye appeal and it was amazing how little change was necessary to translate Harte's sketches into stock shots.

The magazine field today has two of the finest technical craftsmen living working the western fiction lode: Ernest Haycox and Luke Short. Both Haycox and Short could undoubtedly apply their techniques to any field that appealed to them, for they are masters of their craft. This craft is separate and distinct from the fact that they work by choice in the field of the western story.

Perhaps the classic example of two-dimensional grotesquerie in western fiction comes between Harte and Haycox, in the "Wolfville" stories by Alfred Henry Lewis. There is factual foundation for his characterizations; there are grins, chuckles, and even belly-laughs in their actions; there is fine, sensitive, descriptive writing but . . . the finished product is not true to the times, scene, or people that "Wolfville" is supposed to portray. Once you start looking behind the easy entertainment of Wolfville, you find it to be just a painted, property backdrop for a road show company's performance of "The Wild West After Dark," before which backdrop the entire cast sells Kickapoo Snake Oil between acts.

What then composes one man's opinion of the fiction that makes up the only true Literature of the West-That-Was? Well, certain passages from Owen Wister simply because they were first to show that there was something in the native life of the West that would stand on its own feet and make itself a market as fiction. There are some short stories by Stewart Edward White, most of them included in his book *Arizona Nights* and the best of them involving Señor Buck Clark. Then there is George Patullo with, for example, *The Sheriff of Badger, Blue Blazes* and many another. Finally, there are the short stories, novels, and novelettes of Eugene Manlove Rhodes.

In considering the four men named, all of whom have jogged down that trail where the pony tracks point just one way, it is

interesting to note that Wister and White were trained writers
before they came upon the western scene. Yet despite their craft,
or perhaps because of it, they were able to capture something of
the essence of their material and make it palatable to their known
audience demands.

Of George Patullo, I know very little except that his stories are
not only fine writing and good reading, but they ring clear and true
as a shod hoof on *malpais*.

When it comes to Eugene Manlove Rhodes, his process of
translating life into saleable words was just the reverse of Wister's
and White's. Rhodes grew up in New Mexico, was a civilian scout
against the Apache when still in his 'teens, broke horses, worked
cattle, homesteaded, sweat, fought, starved, loved, and lived for
years before he took on the painful task of becoming one of the
finest of Western authors. If you can find his published works, then
you have before you a rare delight in store. There are ten novels
and several essays between covers, plus innumerable short stories,
articles, and verse in magazines. They all are hard to come by and
make a surprising return on investment for the proprietors of
second-hand book stores. They are passionately pursued by an
ever-growing band of followers whom DeVoto describes as being "a
coterie as select and discriminating as any that ever boosted a
tenth-rate English poet into a first-rate reputation."

These are strong words even from a man who is noted for the
pungency, vitality, and frequency of his opinions. Still, they are
more than confirmed by one of Rhodes' friends, a fellow-craftsman
of high renown in the western field, Eugene Cunningham:

> I could write a weighty literary article, à la Lytton
> Strachey, proving by 'Gene's women and playboys that he was
> *not* a mechanic of even tolerable skill: he could *not* create
> people. He could only (and upon my marrowbones I thank
> Mr. Swinburne's Gods for it) *photograph in color, record in
> faintest intonation* real people he knew. Thank the Lord
> again!

Rhodes wrote "westerns"; they appeared in the *Saturday
Evening Post*, which many claim to be the antithesis of true
literature; and yet, in the writings of Eugene Manlove Rhodes is
embodied the true literature of one certain era in the American
pageant. He summed up the code and the creed of his time in many

stories but the fragment that remains ever with me comes from his poem, "The Hired Man on Horseback":

> A brown hand lifted in the splashing spray
>> Sun upon a golden head that never will be gray
> A low mound bare—until new grass is grown
>> But the Palo Pinto trail herd has crossed the Cimarron.

If four lines of poetry can sum up a man, an era, and a creed, let these stand for the last great outpouring of free men's pride in themselves and equal regard for the self-respect of their fellows that made the West-That-Was what it was. This is the basic tenet of the oft despised "western story" and many a school of literature has been built on less.

In the olden days in California, before too many gringos came, it was the custom to give thanks for hospitality regardless of the fare you ate. Then the host or hostess returned the courteous reply that I make here . . . *Buen Provecho!*

11

Prolegomena to the Western

JOHN G. CAWELTI

*John G. Cawelti is professor of English and humanities at the University of
Chicago. He is the author of* The Six-Gun Mystique, *a book on the popular
Western.*

I

Many of my generation doubtless remember bolting dinner and
rushing to the radio to hear the opening bars of Rossini's *William
Tell Overture* followed by the thundering hoofbeats of the great
horse, Silver. Three times a week, year in and year out, the Lone
Ranger rode the radio networks from Station WXYZ in Detroit.
Those of us who were true addicts came to know every conceivable
regularity and variation within the half-hour program format. To
this day, though it has been some 20 years since I last heard the
great cry "Hi-ho Silver" I can still remember the shape of the
program. I believe I could state almost to a minute the time that
elapsed between the opening and the first gunshot, a time that
varied little from year to year. In fact, during the several years of
my regular listening to the masked man's exploits, I can remember
almost no variations in the basic pattern of the program. Everything was precisely worked out from the opening introduction to
the last dying away of the Lone Ranger's voice as he, Silver, and
Tonto rode away after bringing law and justice into the life of still
another Western community. Even a change in commercial
became a noticeable and almost disturbing event in this grand
stylized parade from beginning, through middle, to end. As I recall
my responses to this peculiar work of art, it seems perfectly clear
that the compelling thing about it was not so much the particular
content of any of the episodes—I have long since forgotten what

happened on any particular program and doubt that I even paid much attention to it at the time—but the vigorous clarity and the dynamic but somehow reassuring regularity of the form itself.

The Lone Ranger no longer holds the fascination he once did, but he still interests me in a different way—as a cultural phenomenon of some significance. I am not alone in this, for the scholarly investigation of popular forms like the Western has increased greatly in the last two decades from both humanistic and social scientific points of view. Unfortunately, however, this scholarly investigation has little of the vigorous clarity and precision which often characterizes its subject matter. To examine such a collection as the anthology *Mass Culture*[1] is to realize not only that there is no meaningful consensus about an appropriate method of analysis for popular cultural forms, but that there is not even any significant agreement about what they are. Humanists tend to approach the problem from one point of view, social scientists from another. Nowhere do we find a single set of definitions and assumptions within which the diverse insights and methods of the scholars who deal with popular culture can be meaningfully related to each other.

It is my opinion that these difficulties arise directly from a failure to treat popular cultural forms seriously as what they most obviously are: artistic constructions primarily created and used for aesthetic purposes. In this paper, I wish to explore some of the implications of this proposition. I will begin with a general critique of current approaches to the study of popular forms. Then, confining myself largely to the particular case of the Western, I will try to suggest how we might develop a useful method of analysis. Finally, I will discuss the way in which such an analysis can lead to a fruitful procedure for analyzing the cultural significance of popular forms.

Two assumptions about the character of popular culture have been largely responsible for our failure to develop a coherent conceptual system, agreed on by historians, humanists, and social scientists, for the analysis of popular culture. These are (1) that popular culture is not only qualitatively, but generically different from "serious" culture and that, therefore (2) a work of popular culture should be treated as something other than a work of art; that it must be primarily analyzed as a collection of social themes, a hidden ("latent") work of political rhetoric, a concealed bit of psychoanalysis, or an unconscious religious ritual. Let us examine these assumptions more thoroughly.

1) In the first flush of enthusiasm over the great nineteenth century developments in sociology and naturalistic philosophy, many students of literature and art began to interpret all works in terms of some principle of social determinism.[2] This procedure reached its nadir in the pedantic Marxist criticism of the 1930's, when critics reduced great writers like Henry James to object-lessons of bourgeois decadence and applauded the self-conscious proletarianism of such now-forgotten trivia as Clara Weatherwax's *Marching, Marching.*[3] Practiced by men of broad knowledge and love of the arts the social approach to literature was a liberating force which helped rescue the arts from the doldrums of Germanic scholarship and the formalistic didacticism of Victorian gentility.[4] However, the method of direct correlation between sociological reality and aesthetic expression never established itself as a permanently fruitful basis for artistic analysis. Even in the heyday of the social approach to literature and the visual arts, music was always the odd man out. If the principle of sociological determinants of aesthetic expression was valid, music should have been no different from the other arts, yet it was always evident in this case that a difference in the form and medium of expression vitally affected the method of analysis. In the last two decades, even sociologically oriented students of the arts have reemphasized the independent status of aesthetic expression as a mode of human experience.[5] Though a kind of popular sociologizing and psychoanalyzing persists in the mass media, few serious critics would think of drawing a direct causal connection between some specific social condition or ideology and a novel by Henry James or a painting by Picasso.

However, the tendency toward a simplistic cultural, sociological or psychological reductionism persists unabated in the analysis of such popular cultural forms as the Western because it is easy to assume that the greater simplicity and popularity of such forms reflects a generic difference between the popular work and the more complex serious one. But is a television western really different in kind from any other work of art? Indeed, it is perfectly obvious that the commercial and organizational circumstances under which a television western is produced establish different aesthetic rules and limitations from those encountered by the isolated poet in his garret, or his university office, but why should this lead us to assume that the Western is not primarily an artistic construction similar in nature if not in quality or complexity to a play by Shakespeare or a novel by James Joyce. And if it is an artistic construction, how will we ever arrive at an understanding of its cultural significance by treating it as something else?

2) The consequence of assuming that the popular work is generically different from the serious one is that we must then make it into something other than a work of art. Here we inevitably start riding our own special hobby horses. The theologian sees the Western as a religious ritual, the sociologist as a skirmish in the class struggle, or a hidden bit of political rhetoric, the humanist as a decadent offshoot of some form of traditional culture, the psychologist as a maneuver of the psyche, the anthropologist as a contemporary trope of some primitive myth. We are confronted with an embarrassing wealth of mutually exclusive versions with no way of bringing them together into a single, coherent analysis.

II

An essay on the Western by Mr. Peter Homans suggests a way of resolving some of these difficulties, though, in the end, it too falls into the trap of reducing an artistic construction to a simplistic cultural explanation.[6] Mr. Homans approaches the Western by attempting to understand it as a unified construction before he tries to determine its cultural significance. His method, therefore, involves three main steps: (1) isolation of the characteristic elements—setting, characters, events, themes—of the Western; (2) analysis of the characteristic way in which the Western organizes these elements into an ordered pattern or plot; (3) determination of the cultural significance of this pattern. Using this approach, Mr. Homans concludes that the basic pattern of the Western is a plot "in which evil appears as a series of temptations to be resisted by the hero—most of which he succeeds in avoiding through inner control. When faced with the embodiment of these temptations, his mode of control changes, and he destroys the threat. But the story is so structured that the responsibility for this act falls upon the adversary, permitting the hero to destroy while appearing to save."[7] This pattern, Mr. Homans feels, is related to the cultural

influence of "Puritanism" because it has the same emphasis on the
necessity for inner control and repression of "the spontaneous, vital
aspects of life."[8] The popularity of the Western, therefore, is to be
attributed to its permitting a legitimated indulgence in violence
while reasserting at the same time the "Puritan" norm of the
primacy of will over feeling. Therefore, Mr. Homans believes there
is a connection between the popularity of the Western and the
cyclic outbursts of religious revivalism in the United States.

Despite a number of dubious historical generalizations—a much
oversimplified definition of Puritanism and a questionable dating of
religious revivals, for instance—it seems to me that Mr. Homans'
basic approach is unexceptionable. He recognizes that the Western
is not simply a collection of characters or themes, but an artistic
construction which results in "an ordered vision of character, event
and detail."[9] Furthermore, Homans points out that the analyst
must not only identify typical settings, characters, and events, but
discover and state their relationship to each other in terms of some
"basic organizing and interpretive principle for the myth as a
whole."[10] The analyst must, in other words, define the action or
plot in Aristotle's sense of the term. A statement of what happens,
or a list of characters will not suffice, for events and characters in
any dramatic work cannot be correctly interpreted except in
relation to the structure of the whole work. Many critics point with
alarm to the events of violence which occur so frequently in
contemporary popular cultural forms, but simply to count with
horrified fascination the number of beatings, murders, eye-
gougings, etc. which one can encounter in a day of television
viewing will lead to little in the way of illumination. Imagine what
a viewer-with-alarm might say about a television program which
began with a murder and moved through suicides, poisonings, and
suggestions of incest to end up with the screen littered with
corpses. Pretty terrible, and doubtless indicative of the alienation,
sadism, and nihilism which dominates contemporary popular
culture, except that these events were not taken from a television
Western, but from Shakespeare's *Hamlet*. The point, of course, is
that in an artistic construction, events, even violent ones, take their
meaning from the whole structure. There is quantitatively just as
much violence in Shakespeare or in *Oedipus the King* (a nice bit of
eye-gouging) as there is in *Gunsmoke*, but it does not mean the
same thing. In the Western, violence is characteristically the hero's

means of resolving the conflict generated by his adversary; in Shakespeare it is the means by which the hero destroys himself, or is destroyed; in the classic detective story, violence is the adversary's means of protection and the hero's clue. In each instance, violence cannot be understood simply as violence, for its meaning depends on the place it plays in the overall structure of the action.

Thus, the first step in the cultural analysis of any artistic construction must be the definition of its elements and their relations. In the case of a narrative or dramatic construction like the Western, the elements are characters, events, settings, themes or ideas, and language, and the pattern is that of a plot or action in the sense of a unified chain of events growing out of the motives and ideas of a group of characters and having a definable beginning, middle and end.

Social scientists may well object at this point that the method of analysis I propose is essentially a humanistic approach and is therefore hopelessly subjective and unscientific, for everyone knows that humanists are continually quarreling over the interpretation of the works of art with which they deal. It is true that to isolate and quantify the elements of a pattern is apparently a more scientific procedure than the attempt to define their complex relationships to one another. But, as I have suggested, such a procedure is so false to the nature of artistic constructions that it is about as scientific as it would be to think one had analyzed an election by counting the number of polling places. Nor is the kind of plot analysis I have suggested as subjective as it seems, for there is the direct empirical test of whether the analyst's model of the plot actually fits the work itself, or, to put it another way, whether the suggested organizing principles actually account for the various elements in the work. A good plot model should provide a basis for explaining why each event and character is present in the work, and why these events and characters are placed in the setting they occupy. If some element remains unexplained, it is clear that the organizing principles have not been adequately stated.

III

Mr. Homans' careful discussion of a typical Western plot seems to me an excellent proof that such an analysis can be carried on carefully and objectively. Unfortunately in the case of Mr. Homans' analysis, a confusion between a typical Western plot and *the* Western as a popular form leads to a breakdown in his methodology and finally to an unwarrantedly simplistic conclusion. The reason for this is that there is an important difference from a methodological point of view between *the* Western and say, a novel by Henry James. The latter is a unique construction shaped by a highly individual artist, while the former is a general type with many different particular versions. In studying the cultural significance of a work by Henry James we are dealing with the vision and creative power of a unique individual. In other words, a novel by James is, because of its uniqueness, a type in itself. However, in analyzing a popular form like the Western, we are *not* primarily concerned with an individual work, such as a single episode of *Gunsmoke* or a particular novel by Zane Grey, but with the cultural significance of the Western as a type of artistic construction. This is simply because the circumstances in which a Western is produced and consumed do not encourage the creation of unique individual works of art, but lead to the production of particular realizations of a conventional formula. Therefore the culturally significant phenomenon is not the individual work, but the formula or recipe by which more or less anonymous producers turn out individual novels or films. The individual works are ephemeral, but the formula lingers on, evolving and changing with the times, yet still basically recognizable. Therefore, a popular form, like the Western, may encompass a number of standard plots. Indeed, one important reason for the continued use of a formula is its very ability to change and develop in response to the changing interests of audiences. A form which cannot be adapted like this will tend to disappear. One good illustration of this is the immensely popular nineteenth century form of the moralistic, sentimental novel of seduction which grew out of Richardson's *Pamela*. In the twentieth century the cultural patterns which made this form of narrative meaningful and exciting have changed too much for the form to adapt to them. Other popular formulas, like the Western and the detective story, have thus far proved more adaptable to changing cultural needs.

The trouble with Homans' analysis is that he takes one typical plot for *the* Western. There are many Westerns of the type Homans describes in which an outsider comes into a community, is tempted by evil, overcomes the temptation, destroys the evil and leaves again. On the other hand, there are a good many Westerns in which the central action is the initiation of the hero into the world of men—as in stories of the dude-become-hero variety—or in which the plot hinges on the resolution through violence of a conflict between love and social prejudice—as in Owen Wister's classic *The Virginian*. What we need are plot analyses comparable to those Homans has given us of the several standard Western plots. From such analyses we shall be able to discern more clearly than before the general outlines of the form by discovering those patterns which run through all the types of Western plot. In addition, these plot models would certainly tell us a great deal about the changing significance of the Western, for I have no doubt that, if we were able to classify the types of Western plots, we would find that certain plots have been particularly popular at different times. Being able to trace changes within the form should enable us to discover many important things about changes in the culture which produced it, and there is no better way of defining these changes than through the comparison of plots.

But what of the form itself? What is *the* Western and how can it be objectively defined in such a way that we can relate it to the culture or cultures in which it flourishes? In a sense, *the* Western as a form is simply the sum of the various plots which creators of Westerns have used. Thus, as I have suggested, one way of defining the form is by generalization from careful analyses of the various types of Westerns which have been created. Yet, *the* Western also seems to be something more or at least something different from any or all particular Westerns. Different as they are in characters, events, and even settings, we have no difficulty in recognizing a fundamental similarity between *The Virginian* and *Gunsmoke*. Furthermore, it seems reasonable to predict that if the Western retains its popularity, new versions different in many respects from those known before, yet still recognizable as Westerns, will be developed. It would seem, therefore, that *the* Western is not primarily a set of characters, events and settings, but a set of rules or formulas for shaping many different kinds of material into a certain pattern of experience. If this is correct, a meaningful definition of *the* Western must ultimately take the form of stating, as best we can, a set of rules for the construction of an imaginary world characterized by a certain kind of experience. This fictional world must resemble the world we know at enough points to justify our temporarily accepting it as the real thing. At the same time, however, the world of the formula must have a satisfying clarity and certainty as well as a kind of excitement, suspense, and resolution which remove us from the ordinary world and give us a momentary sense of release from its ambiguities and anxieties. In many ways, it seems to me, the fictional universe of such popular formulas as the Western, the detective story, and the secret agent adventure, resembles the world of a game with its clear opposing sides, restricted patterns of action, heightened suspense and certain resolution in victory and defeat. Perhaps this is why the great spectator sports and the major formula stories form the staples of popular entertainment.

If we follow through the game world analogy, I think we can delineate three central characteristics which most popular formulas must meet:

1) A game must have clearly opposing players—usually, in the large spectator sports, two sides. These form basic moral reference points to which the viewer or participant relates with clearly positive or negative feelings. Similarly in most clearly differentiated popular formulas we have sides: a hero or group of good people and a villain or band of evildoers. The relations between these sides dominate the action. 2) A game has a set of rules indicating which actions are legitimate and which are not; only certain moves can take place and they must happen in a certain order and move toward a particular result. Analogously, a formula story has a particular pattern of expectations. Certain situations occur and others are definitely excluded by the rules. For example, in the detective story the criminal must be detected. To have a still unsolved crime at the end of the book is definitely out of bounds. In the case of the Western, one of the most important rules is that the hero cannot use violence without certain justifications. 3) Finally, a game takes place on a certain kind of board or field whose shape and markings indicate the significance of particular actions. The formula story also depends on a particular kind of setting, an abstracted social structure and landscape which give meaning to particular actions. In this way, the Western hero's relation to the town is analogous to the football player's relation to the line of scrimmage.

Let us now see how these three characteristics might help define the Western formula. First, since a game is basically determined by its board or field, so a popular formula tends to be initially characterized by its setting. Thus, the secret-agent story and the Western differ in that one takes place in a world dominated by the struggle of rival nations and is usually set in a contemporaneous time, while the other unravels itself in an imaginary game world where the fifty yard line is the frontier and the major points of social and geographical topography are an advancing civilization on one side and a savage wilderness on the other. Against this background, a three-sided game is played out. There is the good group of townspeople who stand for law, order, decency, and the whole complex of values associated with civilization; there are the villains who are characterized by their rejection or perversion of these values and by their closeness to the savagery and lawlessness of the surrounding wilderness; and finally, there is the hero whose part is basically that of the man in the middle. Unlike the townspeople the hero possesses or comes to possess the savage skills of violence and the lawless individualism of the villain group, but he is needed by and finally acts on the side of the good group of townspeople. The pattern of expectations which characterizes the Western is too complex to spell out in any detail here, but some of its main lines can be indicated. There must be a series of acts of violence to set the three-sided game in operation and to provoke and justify final destruction of the villain in such a way as to benefit the good group. Usually these acts are worked out in a sequence of chase and pursuit which can make use of the Western field of action and its particular form of movement, the horse, to the greatest extent. Because the crucial result of the game is not the hero's final fate, but the resolution of the conflict between the hero's alienation and his commitment to the good group of townspeople Westerns end in many different ways. Sometimes the hero gets killed, sometimes he rides off into the desert, sometimes he marries the rancher's daughter and becomes a leading citizen. As I have already noted, I suspect that important differences in cultural attitude are indicated by changes in the kinds of plot which are the most popular ways of working out the Western formula at different times. It is no doubt significant that the great majority of Westerns in the first three decades of the twentieth century follow Wister's *The Virginian* in creating plots of romantic synthesis. The typical Zane Grey story or pulp western of the 20s and 30s associated the hero's victory over the villain with his assimilation into the developing society usually by marrying the school teacher or the rancher's daughter. After World War II, however, the most significant Westerns have dealt with the gunfighter. In the typical gunfighter story the hero's violence, though necessary to the defeat of evil, nonetheless disqualifies him for the civilized society which he is saving. Similarly, in this more recent type of Western, the good group of townspeople is usually presented in a far more ambiguous way, as if there were some question whether they merited the hero's sacrifice.

If we turn from the problem of defining the formula to the question of interpretation, we are now in a position to see why this job is so complex and cannot be reduced to a simple psychological or sociological function as for example in the kind of explanation which states that the Western is "a puritan morality tale in which the savior-hero redeems the community from the temptations of the devil" or such a typical psychoanalytic explanation as "the cowboy myth in its form of manifest denial of the female or mother figure represents the intense childhood desire for her and the fears attending these desires, namely that gratifying these wishes carries with it the implication that she is weak and powerless in the face of father." Not that either of these statements is incorrect. In fact, I am inclined to believe that both of them, along with twenty other such statements I could quote, are right, but only partly so. The Western, like any work of art, has many different kinds and levels of meaning. If it did not have a complexity of meanings it could not continue to appeal to so many different groups of people over such a considerable period of time. The real problem is how these levels of meaning are connected with each other. If we can arrive at a better understanding of how popular artistic formulas select and integrate a complex of cultural and psychological meanings into an imaginary world, we will have a better understanding of these popular types than if we look for a single sociological or psychological key. Moreover, I think that seeing how popular formulas synthesize and give pattern to many different themes will give us insight into the way in which our culture organizes and unifies diverse values. For example, the Western certainly addresses itself to the problem of individual spontaneity and freedom in relation to social responsibility and discipline, to the opposition between institutionally defined law and the individual's personal sense of morality and justice, and to the relation between nature and society. The dramatization of these conflicts is one of the signif-icances of the Western field of action and the three-sided game described above. If we consider how the Western articulates these values, certain interesting constellations are revealed. First, there is the assumption that law and individual morality, society and nature, social involvement and freedom are opposing values and that these oppositions parallel each other. Second, the Western formula seems to suggest that these opposing values can and must be resolved, but that the resolution can only occur through violence. I'm not quite sure why this is so, but it seems to have something to do with the nature and role of the villain and the way in which he represents some of the same values as the hero. When the hero finally commits himself to the destruction of the villain, he is destroying an aspect of himself. To do so, he must become convinced that the lawless individualism which the villain represents is so dangerous that it must be completely destroyed. If this analysis is at all correct, it suggests that the Western's resolution of the conflict between society and the individual is one in which society demands the destruction of much that is valuable in the individual self and is yet a necessary and desirable commitment because unrestrained individualism is still more frightening.

I hope that these extremely tentative and incomplete reflections have at least suggested that analysis of a popular formula like the Western is a very complex task. Furthermore, I have sketched in only one dimension of the formula, its treatment of the cultural values of individualism, natural spontaneity and social discipline. Many other areas of meaning remain to be explored and related to each other. In addition, I have not satisfactorily dealt with the problem of different versions of the formula, the way in which it has changed over the last century and a half from the Leatherstocking saga, to Wister and Grey's romantic tales of the hero who becomes fully assimilated into the society, to our present-day fondness for elegaic tales of gunfighters who are sacrificed for a society which no longer has a place for them. These changes as well as the different kinds and levels of meaning in the basic formula need to be explored and defined more carefully if we are to arrive at an adequate cultural interpretation of the Western and other popular formulas.

What needs to be attended to, then, is the serious study of the popular formula as a complex artistic structure with many different levels and kinds of meaning. Once the character of these structures has been more thoroughly and completely defined we need to examine with greater care both the many changes which have taken place in these formulas and the different kinds of meaning which they embody. In addition, I suggest that we undertake to make comparisons between the pattern of the imaginary world which defines the Western formula and the characteristic patterns of other popular forms not only from the arts but from other areas of culture such as sports, politics and manners. If artistic constructions are a way of giving shape or pattern to human experience, it is quite possible that we will find reflections of similar ordering principles in other aspects of the culture. Above all, I feel we must get away from the assumption that an artistic form, even a popular formula is dependent upon some single deeper economic or psychological or social motive, instead of a relatively autonomous means of giving order to a great variety of values and experiences. This is why it is so important to understand a popular formula as an artistic whole. It is the way in which the formula orders and shapes character, action and theme which is of primary importance. If we had a fuller and clearer understanding of the ordering principles which govern the imaginary world of the Western and other popular formulas, we would, I feel, have a better understanding of the patterns of experience which dominate our culture and shape the lives of all of us.

NOTES

1. Bernard Rosenberg and David M. White (eds.) *Mass Culture*, Glencoe, Ill.: The Free Press, 1957.
2. Cf. Hugh D. Duncan, *Language and Literature in Society*, Chicago: University of Chicago Press, 1953, for an extensive bibliography of the sociological study of literary works.
3. The "classic" example of Marxist criticism in the 1930's is Granville Hicks' book on American literature, *The Great Tradition*.
4. Cf. the work of Taine and Brandes in Europe and Parrington in America.
5. An excellent discussion of this point can be found in Lionel Trilling's criticism of Parrington in "Reality in America" reprinted in *The Liberal Imagination*. Both of the two major critical movements of the last two decades, the "New Criticism" of Ransom, Brooks, Warren, Blackmur, *et al.*, and the "Aristotelianism" of Kenneth Burke and the "Chicago school" of McKeon, Crane, Olson, *et al.*, have had as a major principle the integrity and uniqueness of the work of art.
6. Peter Homans, "Puritanism Revisited: An Analysis of the Contemporary Screen-Image Western," *Studies in Public Communication*, no. 3 (Summer 1961), pp. 73–84.
7. *Ibid.*, p. 82.
8. *Ibid.*, p. 83.
9. *Ibid.*, p. 74.
10. *Ibid.*, p. 82.

12

The Practical Spirit:
Sacrality and the American West

MAX WESTBROOK

Max Westbrook is professor of English at the University of Texas, Austin.

The American people are committed to a belief in spirit.[1] From the Puritans to the S.D.S., from the vision of Thomas Jefferson to the grace of John Kennedy, from expansion in the West to the expansion of General Motors, and even in its steady devotion to material goods America has believed that the democratic experiment must count for something more than money, must be based on a value of spirit and not of flesh. We do talk a great deal about sex and money and facts, and in practice our devotion to the spiritual may come closer to betrayal than to devotion; but our most characteristic values—as illustrated by the ideals of the Constitution—suggest a faith in some reality more permanent than the objects and triumphs of the temporal world.

An American spirit, of course, cannot long deny the flesh, the commercial, the efficient world. We believe in ideals but not in the idealized; verbal slashing of the Protestant Ethic is a favorite American sport, but we still want virtue to have its material rewards.

Herein lies an old and frequently-analyzed paradox. In the minds of most Americans, the spiritual and the practical are antagonistic to one another. We tend in fact to associate the spiritual with an impractical and unrealistic type of romanticism, with escapism. When an American dares to speak out for the spiritual values he wants to believe in (and in his own curious way does believe in), he must immediately hide behind patriotism, or make a joke, or break

Copyright 1968 by the Western Literature Association. A paper delivered at the annual meeting of the Western Literature Association, Albuquerque, October 1967. Reprinted from *Western American Literature* 3, no. 3 (Fall 1968) by permission of the author and the Western Literature Association.

a rule of grammar; he must do something to take the taint off, something to make certain no one can accuse him of being *impractically* spiritual, unrealistic about sex and money and facts. With the New Left, the favorite device is the obscene, the four-letter word as instant magic to scare away anyone who might accuse the advocate of love of being unrealistic. Another favorite device, common to a variety of parties, is the firm citation of economic facts. We apologize, in short, for our belief in values of the spirit; and the apology short-circuits our pathetic attempt to believe in permanent values. Let this not be misconstrued (I am putting in my own taint-remover) as an attack on the practical; my point is that we gain little energy from a spirit we are ashamed to have in the house unless it is properly disguised and disgraced.

Our conscious minds are often aware of this cultural awkwardness, and our unconscious minds are aware of it constantly; but we would fain put the blame on someone else, and the favorite scapegoat (rivalled only by the aristocrat and the intellectual) is the Puritan. This little gambit, at bottom, is one of the most deceptive fictions of our psychological history. The Puritan *has* played his part in our cultural schizophrenia, but not in his overpunished and inaccurately represented fear of the practical flesh. It is true that our founding fathers also founded the paradox. It was the Puritan who took the first steps in our continuing effort to bring the eternal into the fold of individual man's concept of democratic justice. In our obsessive rebellion against the Puritan, however, we forget that he was himself a rebel, an honest if bigoted rebel, and that our awareness of his failure does not mean that we are more practical or that the problem has vanished.

Jonathan Edwards, an intensely spiritual Puritan, was at least trying to be practical when he conducted his own version of Kant's Copernican Revolution, his effort to see the absolute from man's subjective viewpoint and thus make it possible to believe that man participates in his own salvation. Edwards wanted to grant the integrity of the individual's psychology, man's personal and subjective status as an observing and feeling individual and yet believe in an absolute that applied equally to all men. The Doctrine of Affections is the means by which Edwards sought to grant God His absolute dominion over salvation while granting also a reality to man's own participation in his election. And it is Edwards' version of the Copernican Revolution that best expresses the Puritan Dilemma inherent in the Doctrine of the Elect.

For the most part, the rest of us have dealt with this problem by not facing it, by exposing the flaw in Puritan thinking rather than by coming up with a better solution. Thus the problem keeps appearing: in Melville's Ahab, who dies in a fanatic attempt to assert his warped affections into an uncompromising absolute; in Hawthorne's Hester, who maintains an integrity of self, an island of identity not quite owned by a God she nonetheless obeys; in Twain's Satan, who represents in a single voice both the absolute which ignores man and the absolute which pays intimate and leisurely attention to individual man; in James's studies of manners and morals, and in Hemingway's symbolic story of Santiago, and in the works of numerous other writers and thinkers. We may avoid a theological formulation, but we cannot avoid the problem itself, the problem of man's notions of free will and the uncooperative authority of God, the problem of individual rights and an absolute right which cannot allow the individual his democratic expectation of a generative capability.

Thus the Puritan Dilemma still confronts us, though in a different form: the typical American is unrelentingly democratic, and yet he believes in a God who is ultimately authoritative. It is troublesome to think of God as absolute—the final sanction of the American dream should be friendly to democracy—but it is simply not possible to conceive of a God who submits to the majority vote or who makes ontological alterations to accommodate someone's single personality. Thus the Doctrine of the Elect still plagues us, despite all the ritual of the taint-remover; for salvation, in its official and in its street-corner formulations, does not seem to accord with the intent of democracy. Democracy must advocate a political state in which all men are free to create their own reward, whereas religion must insist that God created all, including the good or bad will by which men supposedly earn their heaven or hell. And yet, to give up the belief in man's capacity to earn his own salvation is to give up the heavenly sanction of democratic man's belief in the political salvation of its citizenry; and to open the eye of the needle and admit all men to various subjective heavens is to make of religion a relativistic farce.

A primitive religion, by contrast, does not try to subsume God within the domain of man's democratic sense of fair play and free will. The primitive man feels God's presence, alive and thumping in the stomach; and a felt-God does not require the medication of efficient analysis. Those who worship an intellectualized symbol of God, however, grow nervous and shameful about a pagan thumping in the stomach; they ground their belief in personal will, which turns into intellectual analysis, which produces sophomoric questions the intellect is helpless to answer: "What right does any man have to say that *his* version of God is *the* version of God?" The question pre-supposes that God must confine His being within the short fences of man's democratic and intellectual garden of consistency, of fairness to all. Each man must be free to discover his own God. But the Godly thump has no patience with this political blasphemy against a religious ultimate. Our politics invites us to believe that we create our selves, but our religion invites us to believe that God created all; and the dilemma is one of the reasons that our belief in the spiritual comes to be destructively separated from our belief in the practical.

The dilemma of America's democratic sense of the spiritual is also one of the things that wrecked Mark Twain. Consider the following quotation:

I will tell you a pleasant tale which has in it a touch of pathos. A man got religion, and asked the priest what he must do to be worthy of his new estate. The priest said, "Imitate our Father in Heaven, learn to be like him." The man studied his Bible diligently and thoroughly and understandingly, and then with prayers for heavenly guidance instituted his imitations. He tricked his wife into falling downstairs, and she broke her back and became a paralytic for life; he betrayed his brother into the hands of a sharper, who robbed him of his all and landed him in the almhouse; he inoculated one son with hookworms, another with the sleeping sickness, another with gonorrhea; he furnished one daughter with scarlet fever and ushered her into her teens deaf, dumb, and blind for life; and after helping a rascal seduce the remaining one, he closed his doors against her and she died in a brothel cursing him. Then he reported to the priest, who said that *that* was no way to imitate his Father in Heaven. The convert asked wherein he had failed, but the priest changed the subject and inquired what kind of weather he was having, up his way.[2]

When Huck Finn subjects societal values to the democratic test of fair play and practicality, he exposes a bogus humanism and discovers a genuine humanism; but when Twain subjected religious values to the same test—as in the above quotation—the values fell apart. Twain could see the contradiction between man's notions of fair play and a God who was supposed to be omnipotent, omniscient, omnipresent, and benevolent; but he could not find a God other than the one described in the Protestant church, and thus he was ill-equipped to deal with the death and suffering that visited his family and friends.

In his happier days, Twain once made a famous journey to the American West, where he worked and loafed, and where he began his career as a writer. This experience, however, did not include baptism into a tradition which could possibly have rescued him from outrageous and bitter and comic attacks on an absurdity he could never quite dismiss. The American West includes many traditions of course—the nostalgic romanticism of James Fenimore Cooper, the drover's ethic of Andy Adams, the historical traditions of the Indian and the trapper and the mountain man, and so on—but among this number is a very basic tradition which I have called American sacrality.[3] This tradition offers no automatic solution to the problems of good and bedeviled Americans like Mark Twain, nor even to its own problems; but it does describe a practical approach to spirit, and in doing so it offers a healthy alternative which may be more central to the original concept of American democracy than the nervous efforts of those who accepted the Puritan Dilemma, and sought to heal it, without realizing they had already accepted a terrifying error.

Basically, sacrality is a belief in God as energy. The powers which thrive in man and in the universe—the good, the evil, the indifferent—are thought to be the original energies which founded the world. This does not mean that ethical values are lost or that the intellect is deprecated. The emphasis must be placed on energy as *primary*, as a power more fundamental than ethics or the intellect. Once the primacy of sacred energies is granted, the way is cleared for man to bring into full play his local abilities and county values, his intellect and his ethics. Affirmation consists primarily in the belief that a Godly energy can be touched again, tapped anew, at any time; man does not have to lean on his dry, intellectual reading of a past time when God touched the world of ancient ancestors. The sacred man can find his rough and realistic God of energy in the beauty of a lake, the harsh heat of a desert, the blank and haunting eyes of a fresh-killed deer. This discovery, furthermore, is a literal one: the sacred man does not find a *symbol* of God; he finds God. He touches the thing itself. If he has the irrational courage to do this, then he can shape primordial energies in ethical directions. If he lacks this courage, the energy remains, but without direction, having only the pent-up and destructive rage of power betrayed; and a frustrated energy will break out in distorted actions or even in the final distortion: suicide.

I know of no school that adheres to any party line of American sacrality (any writer worth studying is a writer who has his own vision), but the tradition, in its various forms, is widespread in American life and letters, and it does provide an exciting way of confronting a profound and democratic challenge.

Our understanding of American sacrality has been blurred, in part, by the fact that the tradition lacks a clear and academic line of development in intellectual history. By contrast, it is not difficult to trace a tradition from Plato to Kant to Coleridge to Emerson and to latter-day transcendentalists; and there is a definite tradition from Aristotle through various authoritarians and experimentalists and skeptics into contemporary movements like the genre criticism of Elder Olson and Northrop Frye. Sacrality has no such academically established lineage. It owes a great deal to the ancient Orient and a variety of primitive cultures, to C. G. Jung, to ontological mavericks like Nietzsche, and to the American West in its own right. But there is no school, there is no Plato or Aristotle, and those who belong wear different hats and seem, oftentimes, to have no social affinity for one another. A tradition which includes Wallace Stevens and Michael Straight, Walt Whitman and Tom Lea, Thomas Wolfe and Frank Waters, John Steinbeck and Robert Bly, Walter Van Tilburg Clark and Lawrence Ferlinghetti, Frederick Manfred and D. H. Lawrence, Vardis Fisher and James Baldwin, any tradition including such diverse figures is understandably a tradition which is more often mistagged than not.

Even more troublesome is the fact that the characteristic themes of sacrality have no ideological allegiance that comes within the standard formulations of the academy. Consider the following poem by Whitman:

> Facing west, from California's shores,
> Inquiring, tireless, seeking what is yet unfound,
> I, a child, very old, over waves, towards the house of
>   maternity, the land of migrations, look afar,
> Look off the shores of my Western Sea—the circle almost
>   circled;
> For, starting westward from Hindustan, from the vales of
>   Kashmere,
> From Asia—from the north—from the God, the sage, and the
>   hero,
> From the south—from the flowery peninsulas, and the spice
>   islands;
> Long having wander'd since—round the earth having
>   wander'd,
> Now I face home again—very pleas'd and joyous;
> (But where is what I started for, so long ago?
> And why is it yet unfound?)

Here are themes typical of sacrality: (1) the commitment to cyclical time rather than to linear time, (2) the recognition of the continuity of life in its intimate effect on the make-up of the Wise Old Child, (3) the search for the original source. Such themes, however, too easily blur out, at least in the classroom, into gross generalizations. The first and the third are often confused with a Rousseauesque search for romantic purity and innocence, and the middle one—the one about childhood—rings a Platonic bell and thus obscures Whitman's meaning. Lines which would bring these themes into more accurate focus are ignored, or the vital connection, at least, is seldom made. Whitman's Wise Old Child, for example, belongs not to Plato but to the primordial gods of sacrality; his innocence is born of a source which produces also a hot and bestial evil. Such lines as the following (from "Crossing Brooklyn Ferry") take Whitman's romanticism away from Romanticism and toward sacrality:

> It is not you alone who know what it is to be ɛ ɨl;
> I am he who knew what it was to be evil;

I too knitted the old knot of contrariety,
Blabb'd, blush'd, resented, lied, stole, grudg'd,
Had guile, anger, lust, hot wishes I dared not speak,
Was wayward, vain, greedy, shallow, sly, cowardly,
    malignant;
The wolf, the snake, the hog, not wanting in me,
The cheating look, the frivolous word, the adulterous wish,
    not wanting,
Refusals, hates, postponements, meanness, laziness, none of
    these wanting.

Whitman was in a fever to avoid judgments, and the fever cut him off from the symbolic and intuitive discriminations necessary to transcendentalism and from the biological and unjust discriminations necessary to orthodox sacrality; and yet in his ancient honesty before the lust and pettiness of himself Whitman caught one of the essentials of American sacrality: if the evil in man's nature is something for which he must be forgiven, something of which he must be cleansed, then man's values are idealized out of all connection with actual life. This essential of sacrality is what Mark Twain did not learn in his journey to the West: our allegiance to pure values can only be an intellectual allegiance. We cannot worship a pure spirit unless we dishonor the grumblings of our stomachs and the ambition of our hands. If we want a practical spirit, then we must learn to admit, to accept, and even to love the evil that is in all men.

The practical way to handle our evil is to discover its sources; and basically, Whitman proclaims, the source is a misalignment of energies. If we can stop depending on books about the dead but still-worshipped memories of creation, if we can return to the original creation as seen in the cycles of this life, then our spiritual hopes can be grounded where they must be grounded: in an energy so fundamental it constitutes the biology of the soul. Modern man, according to a sacred insurance executive named Wallace Stevens, has failed to constitute himself in the original sources: "The sun no longer shares our works," he writes (in "The Man With the Blue Guitar"), "And the earth is alive with creeping men,/ Mechanical beetles never quite warm." In another poem, entitled "No Possum, No Sop, No Taters," Stevens writes again of man's loss of contact with the original: "He is not here, the old sun,/ As absent as if we were asleep./ The field is frozen. The leaves are dry."

Despite their allegiance to the original sources and despite their love of man's holy and raunchy nature, Whitman and Stevens are significantly different from Western writers in the sacred tradition. Whitman's desire to evoke a feeling of divinity within all men and his desire to become the pied piper of democracy negated an interest in discriminations; there was no place in his vision, for example, for a moral mutation like Steinbeck's Cathy in *East of Eden*, whose deformed soul was certainly an unfair and undemocratic gift from non-Whitmanian gods. And Stevens' recurrent emphasis on the "fiction" of belief diverges from the Westerner's emphasis on a literal rather than a symbolic apprehension of sacred reality. In D. H. Lawrence—the Englishman from Taos, New Mexico—we find a version of sacrality much closer to that of Western writers like Clark, Fisher, Manfred, and Bly.

In a book entitled *Apocalypse*, Lawrence develops forcefully three principles central to American sacrality: (1) man is only partly an individual; more basic is man's collective self, and it is in his role as collective man that he is most likely to shape or to betray primordial energies; (2) all men may be considered equal under a political or ethical ideal, but to give an imagined ontological status to the ideal of equality is to cut one's self off from the existing ontology of the undemocratic primordial; men are simply not equal before the impersonal power of desert, mountain, land, space; (3) the God of the universe, or rather the gods of the universe, must be distinguished from the intellectualized and idealized God of the Bible; the primordial gods do not represent reality; they, in the form of energy, *are* reality.

There may be important connections between these three ideas and many of the folk practices and mores of the American West. The tall tale, when used as a rough kind of lesson; the practical joke, when it has a realistic point; the disaffinity for apologizing: these and other Western traits are at least compatible with the primitive origins of sacred thought and with the tough and impersonal lesson dumbly taught by desert and mountain. More important—and more certain—is the observation that sacred writers tend to feel a respect for nature rather than a romantic love for nature; or the respect, at least, is deeper than the love. The primordial variety of nature does include beauties that are easy to love and a vastness that can pull a man out from the death of turning in on himself, but nature includes also an unfeeling and implacable force which may unfeelingly and implacably beat you to death.

The morality demanded by this beauty and force—when judged by the practical standards of fair-play associated with democracy— is too harsh, especially in its indifference to the good intentions of the individual. Witness, for example, the voiceless demands of nature in Vardis Fisher's *The Mothers*. What is moral, for members of the Donner party, is not what is fair; the moral, rather, is whatever amount of animalism is required for survival against the harsh and unrelenting forces of the primitive world. Frederick Manfred's *Lord Grizzly*, in a general way, is comparable; for Hugh Glass learns, crawling on ground level, the permanent sources of life-energy; and the petty need of revenge in the name of a merely human code becomes not even worth rejecting. To feel in your bones the connection between the irrational variety of your self and the irrational variety of the universe is to achieve your own *figura*, a union of the real and the actual, a unity of the practical world and the world of spirit. This is what the men of modern improvements cannot learn, in Frank Waters' *People of the Valley*, and what Maria, finally, does learn:

> There is nothing ever lost but unreal, evanescent images; nothing ever gained but a perception of the enduring reality behind them. This is difficult to learn. We must first learn that there is only one time, and that it contains all, eternally. Maria, having learned it, was content.[4]

It is this belief in the practical spirit, I think, which prompts Western writers to create scenes in which worshippers of the all-good-and-only-good God are taunted with rough words and embarrassing reminders of man's unholy biology. Such devices, as in Tom Lea's *The Wonderful Country*, are a kind of test. If your God is shamed by the dirt and lust of His own universe, then in what sense is it His universe? In what sense is He God? The real gods, it is felt, include that variety which constitutes the universe; and thus no shame need be felt. It follows a goal, an end, is a pathetic and destructive illusion; and herein lies one of the most fundamental and most practical ideas of sacrality.

To tie yourself to a goal in the future is to cut yourself off from the present, is to predict and to program your own death. There is no end to Manfred's *King of Spades,* not in the sense of goals and fixed borders; nor is there an end to Frank Waters' *The Man Who Killed the Deer* or Clark's *The City of Trembling Leaves.* As Mircea Eliade makes clear in his *Cosmos and History,* the establishment of a goal in a concept of linear time drives man to an intellectual separation of himself from the variety of his present life; and indeed, living for the future—as psychologists and sociologists have told us—is one of the most serious diseases of our age. Again, the typical American concept of practicality—the brisk and business-like establishment of a definite goal—represents a fatally narrow understanding of the practical world.

An energy of terrible power cannot be ignored by a practical man. Manfred, in his version of sacrality, shows us in *King of Spades* what happens when primordial energies are betrayed rather than shaped. Earl Ransom is not wrong to want gold, nor is he wrong to feel the physical and spiritual wonder of his wild and virgin Indian maiden. He knows what he ought to do, and even verbalizes it, just as his mother knows what she should do (smelling an old kinship she is unwilling to admit), just as the father—in his own way—has betrayed into obscenity the primal passions of his youth. To feel guilt for a primal urge is to feel a pathological guilt, and Manfred's Kings are caught in an old card game, trapped between a Puritan death and a destructive lust; and they cannot shape their energies to their ancient and present county of the world. Manfred is writing here of what Clark calls, in his version of sacrality, the "power of the nuclear."[5] It is a power often betrayed by men, forcing the women to bring forth their more immediate and more fundamental contact with primal strength, as in Fisher's *The Mothers* and Steinbeck's *The Grapes of Wrath.*

The power I am describing cannot be captured, of course, in a critical essay. That power can be found in Fisher's *Dark Bridwell,* the scene in which primordial fury moves the four-year-old Jeb to an attack so determined it shames his father into retreat;[6] in Paul Horgan's *Far From Cibola,* the concluding description of Leo's inept and cinematic substitute for primal images;[7] or in Frederick Manfred's *The Chokecherry Tree,* the sacrifice of Hilda to a God Mark Twain and millions of Americans have found unrelated to their most secret and splendid beliefs.[8] A different but also important type of evidence of sacrality is available in John R. Milton's interviews with ten Western novelists. Manfred, in answering the question about his desire to write romantically or symbolically, replies, "No. I just take orders from the Old Lizard,"[9] and nine others, each in his own way, each with his own "difference," express a comparable position. They believe in spirit, but they tie their belief to a practical sense of an old and present land, to a various and primal energy. Wallace Stegner, not included in the Milton interviews, puts it this way in *Big Rock Candy Mountain:*

> A man is not a static organism to be taken apart and analyzed and classified. A man is movement, motion, a continuum. There is no beginning to him. He runs through his ancestors, and the only beginning is the primal beginning of the single cell in the slime. The proper study of mankind is man, but man is an endless curve on the eternal graph paper, and who can see the whole curve?[10]

Lawrence Ferlinghetti, in yet another voice of American sacrality, often writes with ironic humor of primal realities and of our absurd efforts to get the Old Lizard on a television program. The following, from *A Coney Island of the Mind,* is typical:

> I am waiting for the Second Coming
> and I am waiting
> for a religious revival
> to sweep thru the state of Arizona
> and I am waiting
> for the Grapes of Wrath to be stored
> and I am waiting
> for them to prove
> that God is really American
> and I am seriously waiting
> for Billy Graham and Elvis Presley
> to exchange roles seriously
> and I am waiting
> to see God on television
> piped onto church altars
> if only they can find
> the right channel

> to tune in on
> and I am waiting
> for the Last Supper to be served again
> with a strange new appetizer
> and I am perpetually awaiting
> a rebirth of wonder[11]

It may seem perverse of me to suggest a tradition so various that it ranges from cowboy to Beat, but the God people are waiting to see on television, it seems to me, is directly comparable to the God Curt wants to tune in on, via his reason, in Clark's *The Track of the Cat*. The "rebirth of wonder" which Ferlinghetti describes with affirmative irony is directly comparable to the lost wonder of childhood which Paul Horgan pictures so brilliantly in *Things as They Are*.

It is in its more contemporaneous versions, in fact, that American sacrality has taken on a freshness that promises a healthy future for the tradition. The poetry of Robert Bly, for example, reveals a marvelous sense of the joy of immediate things, a vision of the practical spirit occupied and peopled out of modernity, and a bold awareness of the impracticality of establishment values. To close then in what is probably the best way, by letting the writer speak for himself, here is Robert Bly tenderly constructing a scene of terror:

> We are returning now to the snowy trees,
> And the depth of the darkness buried in snow, through which
>   you rode all night
> With stiff hands; now the darkness is falling
> In which we sleep and awake—a darkness in which
> Thieves shudder, and the insane have a hunger for snow,
> In which bankers dream of being buried by black stones,
> And businessmen fall on their knees in the dungeons of
>   sleep.[12]

NOTES

1. For a distinguished essay on the subject, see William G. McLoughlin, "Pietism and the American Character," *American Quarterly*, XVII (Summer, 1965), pp. 163–186. Further support is found, from a wide variety of approaches and in a wide variety of topics, in Joseph J. Kwiat and Mary C. Turpie, eds., *Studies in American Culture* (Minneapolis, 1960),

University of Minnesota Press; see especially John W. Ward's "The Meaning of Lindbergh's Flight," pp. 27–40.

2. *Letters From the Earth,* Bernard DeVoto, ed. (New York, 1962), Harper and Row, p. 36.

3. In a book on Walter Van Tilburg Clark. See also my "Conservative, Liberal, and Western: Three Modes of American Realism," *The South Dakota Review* (Summer, 1966), pp 3–19.

4. *People of the Valley* (New York, 1941), Farrar and Rinehart, p. 308.

5. *The City of Trembling Leaves* (New York, 1945), Random House, Chapter XXI.

6. *Dark Bridwell* (New York, 1931), Houghton Mifflin Company, pp. 130–131.

7. *Far From Cibola* (New York, 1938), Harper and Brothers, p. 162.

8. *The Chokecherry Tree* (Denver, 1961), Alan Swallow, p. 34.

9. John R. Milton, ed., "Symposium: The Western Novel," *The South Dakota Review* (Autumn, 1964), pp. 3–36, p. 7 for the specific quotation.

10. *The Big Rock Candy Mountain* (New York, 1957), Sagamore Press, p. 436.

11. Lawrence Ferlinghetti, *A Coney Island of the Mind* (New York, 1958), New Directions Books, pp. 49–50.

12. *Silence in the Snowy Fields* (Middletown, Connecticut, 1946), Wesleyan University Press, p. 25.

13

The Petrified West and the Writer

DAVID LAVENDER

David Lavender, who recently retired from teaching at the Thacher School, Ojai, California, is the author of many distinguished books on American history, including Bent's Fort, Land of the Giants, *and* California: Land of New Beginnings.

As a believer in the literary possibilities of a Yoknapatawpha County in the high plains or Rocky Mountains, I sometimes despair. Can literature about the American West ever be liberated? I am not referring to the historiography of the frontier, where notable work is being done by such practitioners as Ray Allen Billington, Dale L. Morgan, William Goetzmann, and others. I am not referring to novels like Steinbeck's *Grapes of Wrath* that are laid in the West but are not essentially of the West. What I mean are the foredoomed attempts to clear away the connotations clustering around the word "Western" and, that done, to bespeak the frontier's realities in its native idiom—to create, in short, a Literature, capital "L." There is a seemingly immovable barrier, in spite of what novelists A. B. Guthrie, Jr., and Wallace Stegner, poet Thomas Hornsby Ferril and a few others have shown can be done.

The blockade, a familiar monolith vaster than Hoover Dam, is the stereotype now known as the horse opera. Its geographic heart is a warped tele-vision of that dry, luminous land where the high plains lap up against the foothills of the Rockies. Its characters are the people who are reputed to have once lived there. The stereotype is so pervasive that to most readers "American Indian" does not suggest the canoe people of the Eastern forests, the sedentary pueblo dwellers of the Southwest, or the amazing woodworkers of the Northwest; it means, invariably, the be-feathered nomads of the semiarid plains, astride their barebacked ponies. In the national consciousness, Western animals mean the animals of the plains and Rockies—the coyote, the bison, occasionally the grizzly bear. The compulsion once reached to our coins; the head of a plains Indian graced our pennies, a buffalo grazed across our nickels. Although a wagon freighter, cavalryman, prospector, or even lumberjack may on occasion wander through our notions of the frontier, the commanding figure remains the cowboy, or at least a sheriff who once operated as a cowboy. His emblems, unlike those of any other vanished tradesmen, can be listed by 200,000,000 Americans: a horse with its suggestions of knight-errantry, a pair of chaps with their suggestion of armor, a redhot pistol, suggesting, the Freudians say, an unconquerable virility.

Historically speaking, the Man on Horseback rode into this eminence quite understandably. What was to be his first home, the dime novel, attained its tremendous popularity among the bored infantrymen of the Civil War. Immediately after the war, while hundreds of thousands of people still had the habit of reading dime novels, the cattle industry began its spectacular boom, carrying with it illusions of freedom and controllable destiny. Scenting the appeal, Mr. Beadle's hired help quickly transformed the forest pathfinder, bequeathed them by James Fenimore Cooper, into a cowboy and followed the popular imagination into newer, wider spaces. The newcomer sold. He moved into the pulp magazines and did so well there that craftsmen more skilled than the pulpsters—Owen Wister, Emerson Hough, Zane Grey, Eugene Manlove Rhodes—accepted the genre, refined it, and lifted it into middle-class respectability in the pages of the *Saturday Evening Post*. From there to Hollywood was then but the shortest of gallops.

Formulas petrified, time stood still, regional distinctions eroded into smooth conventions. Since for a century readers and now viewers have wanted no fundamental change, neither have editors. They reject and accept by pattern. Critics respond as automatically as moles to whatever suggests "Western" to them. I know of one historically accurate novel of the mining country that was brushed off by a columnist not because of defects it may well have had in plot, style, structure or characterization, but because there were people in it who rode around on horseback; hence it was "Western." (How else should they have journeyed in 1880?) This same novel returned from Hollywood, not with a reason but with a catch phrase: "The West has already been won." There is nothing more to say—unless it is said by rote, in which case the tale can be repeated endlessly.

This kind of foolishness has inevitably had a disastrous effect on what might have been a strong native literature. Writers whose imaginations have been fired by the drama inherent in the actual West recoil in various ways from the shadow of the unreal West. Bernard DeVoto, far and away the most literate of the recent students of the frontier, reacted by fleeing. Declaring flatly that a good story about cowboys could not possibly be written, he turned his back and devoted himself, in nonfiction, to other phases of the nation's westering. More stubborn souls, declining to abdicate the cow country and some of its vital themes, have also buckled on the shield of nonfiction, as Helena Huntington Smith did recently in *The War on Powder River,* an account of the clash between cattlemen and sodbuster-rustlers in Johnson County, Wyoming. It's a worn wheeze, that theme, and Miss Smith's nonfiction at times seems to be employed as a charm for warding off the curse of phoniness, a sort of desperate cry to the reader, Don't leave yet; I know what you are thinking, but this tale is documented, this one is honest.

It is my opinion that somewhere in the land there are writers capable of producing not stereotypes, but imaginative works about the American West. This is a call to them—foredoomed perhaps like Roland's cry at Roncesvalles, or perhaps even faintly comic like outdated Eben Floods's monologue in E. A. Robinson's poem, old Eben alone on a hillside with only his jug and two moons listening. But if someone else should also be listening, then with the call comes warning. Many sirens sing along the Western trails. Unless one is wary when he hears them, he will soon find himself strangling in the very quagmires he had hoped to avoid.

The most alluring of the seductions, superficially at least, is the Western costuming. The deeper the researcher digs for authentic data, the more enthralled he grows. Let me quote, in illustration, six examples from three different Colorado mining camp newspapers of the 1880's. Each of the examples is, in its way, almost irresistible, and each could be multiplied almost endlessly.

The first is from the Aspen *Times* of September 12, 1885.

The usually quiet camp of Aspen was thrown into a state of

excitement yesterday by a difficulty on Aspen Mountain, in which a man named McDowell got a severe blow across the face with an ax-handle & another named Billy Madigan got a bullet in the left shoulder. McDowell told the *Times* reporter, "I . . . was going back to the hundred-one mine, where I am foreman. I was driving a jack and had a 16-foot piece of pipe which I was taking up to the mine. I heard someone behind me . . . turned around and saw Billy Madigan coming up to me. He said "I understand you called my father a gray-haired son of a bitch and I am going to lick you." I said, "No, I don't think I said anything of the kind; but I did say he was an old stinker, and you are another; you are a fine hair, you are." Madigan then said, "I am going to lick you, you s.o.b." "I am going to kill you," I replied. "Throw down your ax-handle and square yourself." Instead, he struck me a terrible blow with the ax-handle on the left side of the head, knocking me down and cutting a gash from which the blood ran down my face. He continued striking at me when I drew my gun and fired one shot in the air. He did not desist and I fired again, striking him as I am told in the left shoulder.

Men in the West were, as the saying goes, men. Let us move on to the women and another excerpt from the Aspen *Times*, this one dated June 18, 1885.

Yesterday morning between 2 and 3 o'clock, just after the Aspen Theater had finished its regular program . . . an additional scene was enacted savoring of tragedy. Julius Benner was the piano player. Maud Lamb, one of Leadville's estrayed citizens, was his solid girl and was jerking beer in the parquette of the theater. Maud had complained that Julius spent his money and more of hers than was proper. When the theater closed, they had a racket among the chairs, which served Maud as instruments of warfare. Soon after, Julius was standing by the bar in the front room taking a drink, when . . . Maud entered with an open jack-knife partly concealed in her hand . . . and stabbed him the stomach, and as she was making other strokes at him he knocked her down, when the deputy marshal arrested them. Benner said, "Hold on till I show you something," and backing up against the wall he pulled up his shirt, showing blood flowing freely from a savage wound in his abdomen clear to his bowels. . . . As Benner declined to prosecute, the officer preferred a charge of drunk and disorderly. She pleaded guilty and was fined $5 and costs.

For a slightly different tone, let us consider a run of events in 1881 in Durango, Colorado, as reported by the editor, who chanced to be a woman, a Mrs. Romney. First an editorial that appeared in the *Record* on March 12 under a heading "Wanted in Durango":

> We want girls! Girls who can get themselves up in good shape to go to a dance . . . girls who will go to church and to Bible-class on Sunday . . . and who will take a buggy ride after the lesson is over. They will help the livery business, and will also hasten the sale of residence lots, for buggies are the vehicles where homes are first thought of by many people. . . .
>
> We want girls for sweethearts, so that when we get an arm shot off, or are kicked by a mule, or thrown from a bucking horse and are laid away for repairs, we may hear a gentle voice and see the glitter of a crystal tear. . . .
>
> We want fat and funny girls to make us smile all over, and lean and fragile ones to hang upon our arms, and petite blondes who show themselves on sunny days; and stately brunettes, so beautiful in the twilight.
>
> We have mineral enough, and plenty of coal, and oxide of iron. The only lack of our resources is those potent civilizers of their pioneer brothers—the girls!

In spite of the wistful appeal, it would appear that there were at least a few potent civilizers in Durango, for a month later, on April 9, the *Record* announced a grand ball to celebrate the opening of the West End Hotel:

> The opening dinner will be spread in the mammoth dining hall from seven to nine pm when an elegant menu . . . will be raided by Durango's elite. After the royal gorge has taken place, the large force of attendants will spirit away the china and broken-hearted champagne bottles, and Professor Deluis and his True Fissure Orchestra will take possession of one end of the room. Then sweet perfumes will greet grateful nostrils, and exquisite strains of Terpsichorean musical messages will

be telephoned through auricular drums, past palpitating
hearts, to agile feet which will not rest till morn.

Unfortunately, a bunch of feuding cowboys shot up the hotel, and
the grand opening had to be postponed. However, there were other
diversions. A vigilante committee lynched one of the brawlers, and
a week later, on April 16, the editor found solace in wielding her
pen over this:

> And a ghastly sight it was. . . . A slight wind swayed the
> body to and fro. The pale moonlight glimmering through the
> rifted clouds clothed the ghastly face with a ghastlier pallor.
> The somber shadows of the massive foliage seemed blacker
> than the weeds of mourning; and the shuffling of hurrying feet
> in the dusty road, mingling with the weird whistling of the
> breeze through the pine boughs broke upon the ear with a
> sepulchral tone. . . . Thus the Powers that Be . . . have
> proclaimed to the world that good order, peace, quietude and
> safety must and shall prevail in Durango.

And finally, for a description of another social phenomenon, let
us turn to Leadville and an undated excerpt from the Leadville
Democrat, as quoted by George Willison on pages 189–90 of his
book, *Here They Dug the Gold.*

> "HELL ON THE ROAD—FIGHTING ALL ALONG THE
> BOULEVARD," read the *Democrat* one morning. "Sunday is
> always an occasion for fast women, rapid men, and all the
> sporting fraternity to air themselves on the beautiful drive.
> Toward evening these cheerful souls got hilarious. Presently,
> some big double-decked rooster opened the ball by jumping at
> a small courtesan and smashing her nose. The matinee then
> began. One female armed herself with a beer bottle and
> created on the head of a well-known gentleman several bumps
> not down on his phrenological chart. He retaliated by taking a
> board and damaging her some. Scarcely was this over when
> another woman drew a revolver and began scattering galena
> around in a particularly reckless fashion, and was only
> induced to stop when her solid man seized her by her false
> hair and mopped up the boulevard with her. Her yells had
> barely died away when another circus performance opened.
>   "We regret to announce that nobody was killed."

All this is delightful stuff, quaint and colorful. Mesmerized by it, one can pretend to hew significant themes out of it. Billy Madigan and his ax-handle and Maud and her jackknife might be classed, for instance, as stories of the unbridled individual in an unsophisticated society where traditions about acceptable behavior have not yet coalesced enough to enforce conformity; the denouement, of course, would then revolve about the refining of the wild. For society did yearn to be tamed, as Mrs. Romney showed in her elegant forecast of the Grand Ball that was to mark the opening of the West End Hotel. And when the opening had to be postponed because of an outbreak of violence, the more stalwart arms of Civilization, the Powers that Be, arose in their wrath and restored order in classic fashion—the vigilante committee.

It is difficult to convince devotees of horse opera that material as entrancing and as seemingly authentic as all that provides sleazy fabric for stories and that in trying to stitch tales out of it they are confusing the costume with the body. Yet these same devotees seldom suppose that contemporary literature (save in the case of lynchings, of which more hereafter) can be tailored out of the similar street brawls that are drably and regularly recorded on the police blotters of every large city. For, you see, the devotees have been accidentally seduced by frontier journalists. These were hardworking men who had little of significance to write (there were also other motivations but there is no space to elaborate on that point) and who therefore clothed the small violences around them with what today seems a fresh and racy vocabulary, ballooned the events onto the otherwise blank front pages, and in so doing unintentionally left behind an impression that almost mindless violence was a primary facet of Western living. Those who are trapped by this into writing about mindlessness naturally feel that they need plumb no deeper than the motions it caused. And so the quagmire closes in, for almost mindless motion is, of course, the chief hallmark of horse opera.

Another seduction in Western writing is the land itself. Its deserts, mountains and canyons are bold and dramatic. The very leap of their lines suggests that certainly they should be the home of men bold enough to match the mountains; they should produce, through some process of self-generation, dramatic episodes. "Great things are done where men and mountains meet," poet William Blake wrote a hundred and fifty years ago. "This is not done by jostling in the street." And so we come to Jack London and London's dog Buck who, in answering the call of the wild, becomes a superdog, and to Smoke Bellew in London's novel of the same name. In San Francisco's jostling streets Smoke is a useless wastrel. But he has superior, Nordic genes in his chromosomes, and the moment he hits the Klondike mountains he becomes, by simple horse-opera biologies, a prodigy of strength and valor.

The romanticism that fathers this sort of plot is apparently ineradicable. I have a deep admiration for Justice William O. Douglas, and especially for his stalwart efforts to conserve the physical grandeurs of the Western landscape. Yet Douglas was able to write in *Of Men and Mountains,* "I have never met along the trails of the high mountains a mean man, a man who would cheat and steal. Most men who are raised there or who work there are as wholesome as the mountains."

The remark started a chain of reflections. The first was a memory of rounding a clump of trees beside a Rocky Mountain trail and coming across a man who, in solitude, had performed the considerable physical feat of roping a wild cow, throwing her, and tying all four of her feet together. He was passionately beating off her horns with a club. She had endeavored to hook his horse, he said, and he was teaching her a lesson. But, then, this was in the Rockies and Justice Douglas was writing of the Cascade Mountains of Oregon.

That roused a second memory, of H. L. Davis' Pulitzer prize-winning picaresque novel, *Honey in the Horn,* in which much of the action transpires in the Cascades. Clay Calvert, the mountain-raised hero of *Honey in the Horn,* smuggles to his jailed stepfather a gun that won't work in hopes that his stepfather will be killed when he tries to use it. The scheme misfires, however, and the stepfather, wrathful now, escapes. Clay has to flee for his life over the wholesome high trails. His companions are a horse-trader for whom the word "mean" is a gross understatement, and the horse-trader's daughter, who without benefit of wedlock supplies the novel with some of its romantic interest. In their wanderings, zestfully told in the racy idiom of the country, Clay and the girl meet a variegated lot of characters who are not only willing to steal and cheat, but eager. Which is the fiction, one wonders: Davis' book or Douglas'?

Another seduction, insidious because of the halftruths it sings, is the notion of the second chance, of a remaking, of a savior who will put the world to rights. The frontier, which once began at the Atlantic seaboard, has always been symbolic of that untrammeled place where the ideals of human dignity can be realized afresh. "Westward," Thoreau said, "I go free." Hoping momentarily to escape from the despair into which her unyielding Puritan society had plunged her, Hester Prynne in *The Scarlet Letter* asked her lover in what is really a plea, "Whither leads yon forest track?" Surely there is something better out beyond. Songs caught the mood: "O Susannah, don't you cry for me!" Willa Cather felt it in such novels as *O, Pioneers* and *My Ántonia,* where the daughters of immigrant farmers, the continuity of their cultures snapped almost overnight, searched for and found the stability they needed in the soil itself.

A tremendous hope went westward with our people, and often only a tremendous disillusionment awaited them. It is in dealing with this disillusionment that writers about the West have come closest to creating an enduring literature. Out on the measureless Dakota prairies, Per Hansa of Rölvaag's *Giants in the Earth* feels clear into his bones the strength of the land for which he is so hungry. But to his wife those same blank prairies offered, in her words, no shelter behind which life could hide; and the emptiness pressed onto her until, for a time, she lost her mind. Comparable themes occupied Hamlin Garland and Ruth Suckow in their bleak descriptions of the stultifying toil that pioneering demanded. For Frank Norris in *The Octopus* America's greedy industrialism was the villain, strangling the wheat that was his symbol of life.

Another Western disillusionment was found in the vitiation of energy. "The lusty pioneer blood is tamed now, broken and gelded," are the opening words of Conrad Richter's *The Sea of Grass.* The conflict of Richter's story arises when nesters—that is, farmers—move onto the New Mexico range of cattle baron Jim Brewton (much as they moved onto the range of the Wyoming barons in Helena Smith's nonfiction *The War on Powder River*). Television screens resound with similar clashes, but in TV it is mere resonance. Richter, however, writing fiction, manages better than nonfiction accounts do to catch the universal tragedy of lost strength: Samson undone by treachery. The nesters, led by a man named Brice Chamberlain, defeat Brewton not directly but by political maneuvers and legal trickery. At the same time, and symbolically enough, Chamberlain seduces Brewton's wife, and the story becomes one of bafflement, of a sad clinging to illusion, until Brewton, tamed now and broken, makes his last bleak compromise with reality.

Something of the same thought is present in Willa Cather's *A Lost Lady*. The lady is lost not because of her unfaithfulness to her railroad-building husband but because she has no focus for her energies, no creative dreams to absorb her vitality. And so, one way or another, the primal energies thin down, the characters turn soft, the towns become—I take the words from the opening sentence of *A Lost Lady*—"those gray towns along the Burlington railroad, which are so much grayer today than they were then."

More than anything else, the horse opera declines such disillusionments. There must be a savior.* It is a sound and honorable theme, of course, as old as Greek Odysseus sweeping with drawn bow on the suitors who have invaded his home and setting both the home and all Ithaca once more to rights. American writers have given this plot some strange twists. As Charles Rolo has pointed out, one perversion of it is Mickey Spillane's sadistic, once-popular solver of problems, detective Mike Hammer. Dress Mike over in woolly chaps, repress his more blatant glandular drives, relocate him in the sagebrush, and what have you got? The cowboy savior, that's what, making the ever-new West safe for man's old dreams.

The prototype is Owen Wister's *The Virginian*. In person the Virginian is, and I quote Wister verbatim, "as beautiful as pictures" . . . Smile when you call me that! But he has a drollery to him, and for a while the book floats pleasantly along through a series of practical jokes, tall tales, even an Indian ambush. Then Eden is invaded by serpents—cattle rustlers. Sadly but efficiently the Virginian hangs all but the head serpent, Trampas, who escapes. Conventional society promptly voices its protests at the extralegal executions through the voice of a schoolma'am named Molly, a strayed chip off an old Vermont block and the Virginian's sweetheart. Molly is, if I may be given the liberty, briefly mollified when the Virginian's boss explains that wherever public law proves weak, private law must step into the breach. But then her standards suffer further strain. In order to keep his manhood unsullied, the

---

*Curiously, the Transmississippi West seems to have produced no truly prophetic novels, no voices crying salvation in the wilderness. Yet it is a logical site for such a novel; both California and Colorado (to say nothing of Mormon Utah) were dotted with utopian colonies, some successful, led by zealots burning with the truth.

Virginian walks down a lonesome street and outguns Trampas in the best *High Noon* style. Molly senses that this is not quite the way in which differences were settled back in old Vermont. She starts another protest. By this time, however, Mr. Wister is handling a very hot potato. Rather than juggle it longer, he lets love conquer even doubt. In her relief at having her man return alive, à la Odysseus, Molly falls weeping onto his chest, and all ends blissfully on an island in a river. The fundamental problems of justice are not faced. They are never faced in "Westerns" or among minute men with horse-opera mentalities. It is enough to be saved, no matter what is lost in the process.

Of course there were lynchings in the West, as there have been everywhere. The classic case, spawner of dozens of yarns, is that of Henry Plummer, who, while serving as sheriff of both Bannack and Virginia City, Montana, secretly led a gang of highwaymen responsible for murdering a reputed one hundred and two people. I do not believe the figure, but no matter; it is only costuming anyway. The body of the matter lay in the formation of a vigilance committee to restore order.

As these self-constituted lawmen of Virginia City were riding forth on their errand, they encountered a hoodlum named Erastus Yeager, better known as Red. Red was tried—no outsider ever knew of what the trial consisted—and was induced to confess—no one ever knew how. He was then executed before the men he had accused could confront him. That done, the vigilantes swept on through the countryside, hanging the men Yeager had named without corroboration to trees, rafters, corral gates, any upright that was handy.

These events occurred late in December, 1863, and early in January, 1864. For one hundred years since then the same apology has been repeated over and over: inasmuch as crooks controlled the apparatus of law enforcement, what other recourse did honest men have?

The rhetorical question prompts another in retort: What else did they ever try? Might there be a story in someone's standing up to voice a protest? But no, the leaning gallows, the whistle of wind through the lonesome places, the grim march of the defenders to the place of retribution—the costuming always wins. And yet, two lawyers in Virginia City did raise the issue of trial by jury and were told by the vigilantes either to keep quiet or leave. Why is that footnote always overlooked?

I know of only one searching novel about a Western lynching, Walter Van Tilburg Clark's *The Ox-Bow Incident,* and it is content with the obvious theme, the possibility that self-directed avengers might in their righteousness be wrong and execute innocent men. There is room for other themes. When Henry Plummer died at rope's end in Bannack, the American Bill of Rights had been in force for seventy-two years. By now, one hundred and seventy-seven years have passed, which is long enough, it would seem, for certain rights to have become traditions of our time. And when suddenly the times were out of joint, was there in those desolate mountain places no Hamlet frozen with horror at what he was being called on to do? No Brutus, lured on to disaster by his own lofty idealism?

A Macbeth existed, I think. Although the point is seldom dwelt on in tales about Plummer, there lived in Bannack during those times one Sidney Edgerton, Abraham Lincoln's appointee as chief justice of Idaho Territory. (Montana in 1863 was a part of newly created Idaho.) Edgerton's nephew, Colonel Wilber F. Sanders, was one of the moving spirits of the vigilantes, albeit he seems to have stayed behind when they went on their rides. Justice Edgerton, surely a representative of the law that is said not to have existed, knew perfectly well what his nephew and the other vigilantes were up to. He uttered no protest, however. Instead he went to Washington and urged that Montana be established as a separate territory, partly on the grounds that law and order would be better served by a division from Idaho. Congress acceded, and when Lincoln selected a governor for the new territory, it turned out to be—that's right—Sidney Edgerton. So perhaps there were witches whispering of ambition across the caldron. Yet all we hear is that vigilantes did only what they had to do in order to preserve fundamental values.

The tale that needs writing is not the one about gangs who kill one hundred and two people nor about the pursuit of such gangs nor about the hanging of their leaders. That's the motion. The story lurks in whatever it was that flickered behind the eyes of the men who did the executing or who declined to do it—a story of frightened men who had followed a gleam of hope from familiarity into strangeness and who one day raised their heads from their digging to find that the traditions and customs by which they had long abided were suddenly gone. Only blind luck remained. The next turn of the shovel might make them wealthier than they had ever before dreamed of being. Or they might starve. But you cannot punish chance. All you can punish, vicariously enough in your reading sometimes, is the threat you can see, the Plummers of the world. And so you assert yourself. Who are you? Ah, you are the savior. Marching with the vigilantes, you grasp for your integrity through emptiness and you catch . . . what?

It's a marvelous story, really. Someday it should be told.

This brings us to the final stumbling block, the problem of relevance. As one drives across the plains and comes abruptly onto the new industrial cities that are rising dramatically against the backdrop of the Rockies—Great Falls, Montana, say, or Denver or Colorado Springs—the notion of finding pertinence in what happened there during a different century seems all at once absurd. And when one drives on into the high country and sees the summer carnival towns—Central City west of Denver or reconstructed Virginia City in Montana—and when one watches the tawdry make-believe with which they try, for the price of a tourist's dollar, to revivify what they all call in capital letters The Old West, the idea of a literature out of such materials seems doubly frantic.

But such hesitations miss the point. There are other relevancies for writing than contemporaneousness. The possibility of being dated never bothered Homer or Shakespeare or, to an extent, Faulkner. They were dwelling on themes that could be enlarged most fully by turning from modernity to mythic periods—periods when, the reader is ready to believe, life was lived according to its elements, when there were no limits to what could be achieved, and when, accordingly, there were also completely wanton freedoms of impulse and passion; when crime grew enormous not by statistic but by its unrestrained denial of the calls of humanity—a time when standards were changing as rapidly as they are now; when fatalism seemed, as it does today, the only possible explanation for the disasters that befall men; when naked self-love openly challenged self-command for supremacy; when King Lear's daughters could, as their heirs do now, tear out eyes without the least twinge of conscience—and when the response to all this is created page by page in the hearts of readers who see in the shadows of that gigantic past the universal present.

   The violent West is America's mythic land. Someday some young writer who does not flee from its stereotype as DeVoto did, who does not feel he must always seek the shield of literalness, and who refuses to yield to the seductions along the way, will see it so, and then with hard granitic style will dig it free from beneath the ash heaps of a century of foolish composition.